BASIC

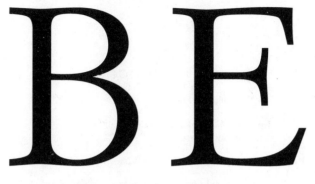

BASIC

BELIEVING THE SIMPLE TRUTH OF GOD'S WORD

OT COMMENTARY

GENESIS 1—11

Warren W. Wiersbe

DAVID C COOK

transforming lives together

BE BASIC
Published by David C Cook
4050 Lee Vance Drive
Colorado Springs, CO 80918 U.S.A.

Integrity Music Limited, a Division of David C Cook
Brighton, East Sussex BN1 2RE, England

The graphic circle C logo is a registered trademark of David C Cook.

Unless otherwise noted, all Scripture quotations are taken from the King James Version
of the Bible. (Public Domain.) Scripture quotations marked NASB are taken from the
New American Standard Bible, © Copyright 1960, 1995 by The Lockman Foundation.
Used by permission; NIV are taken from the *Holy Bible, New International Version*®.
NIV®. Copyright © 1973, 1978, 1984 International Bible Society. Used by permission of
Zondervan. All rights reserved; and NKJV are taken from the New King James Version.
Copyright © 1982 by Thomas Nelson, Inc. Used by permission. All rights reserved.

Library of Congress Control Number 2009934566
ISBN 978-1-4347-6635-9
eISBN 978-1-4347-0090-2

First edition of *Be Basic* by Warren W. Wiersbe published by Victor
Books® in 1998 © Warren W. Wiersbe, ISBN 1-56476-593-8

The Team: Karen Lee-Thorp, Amy Kiechlin, Sarah Schultz, Jack Campbell, and Karen Athen
Series Cover Design: John Hamilton Design
Cover Photo: Veer Inc.

Printed in the United States of America
Second Edition 2010

16 17 18 19 20 21 22 23 24

040822

CONTENTS

The Big Idea: An Introduction to *Be Basic* by Ken Baugh 7

A Word from the Author...11

1. BC: Before Creation (Genesis 1:1) 15

2. When God Speaks, Something Happens (Genesis 1) 27

3. First Things First (Genesis 2).. 39

4. This Is My Father's World—or Is It? 53

5. Perils in Paradise (Genesis 3) 67

6. In Center Stage—Cain (Genesis 4:1–24) 81

7. When the Outlook Is Bleak, Try the Uplook (Genesis 4:25—6:8) .. 93

8. One Man's Faith, One Man's Family (Genesis 6:9—7:24) 105

9. The God of New Beginnings (Genesis 8)......................................117

10. To Life! To Life! (Genesis 9:1–17) 129

11. The Rest of the Story (Genesis 9:18—10:32)...............................141

12. Caution—God at Work (Genesis 11) 153

13. Back to Basics (Review of Genesis 1—11) 163

Notes 173

THE BIG IDEA

An Introduction to *Be Basic*
by Ken Baugh

Everything in this life has a beginning. My ten-year-old car at one time rolled off the assembly line brand spanking new. Many successful entrepreneurs began their businesses in their garages. A professional basketball player doesn't just appear on the court out of nowhere; his or her career begins with the first bounce of a basketball. The Civil Rights movement began as a dream in the hearts of a few determined people. Every marriage had a first date, and every person began his or her life journey at birth.

Everything in this life has a beginning, and so does the Bible: Genesis is the book of beginnings. In the first eleven chapters we discover the beginning of the universe, the earth, human life, sin, death, and redemption. But most important, we discover the beginning of God's love affair with humanity. The apostle John tells us, "God is love" (1 John 4:8). Not simply that God has love, or that God performs acts of love, although these are both true. There is something more basic and fundamental that we must understand about God's nature and character: God *is* love. God is the source and standard of love, and everything God does is motivated by love. He cannot act in any way that is not loving.

Think of it like this: If you release a bird into the air, it flies. Why? Because that's what birds do. If you put a fish into water, it swims. Why? Because that's what fish do. When God creates a universe with human beings, He loves them. Why? Because that's what God does. God loves because God is love. And God's love affair with men and women is the "Big Idea" that runs throughout the first eleven chapters of Genesis. As you read these chapters, you will discover the three dimensions of God's love for people.

Dimension 1: Creation. Humans are unique in all of God's creation, including angelic beings, in that God created only humans in His image: "Let us make man in our image, in our likeness.... So God created man in his own image, in the image of God he created him; male and female he created them" (Gen. 1:26–27 NIV). God made humans like Himself in some crucial ways, so humans are unique and special to God. Humans have intrinsic value, because we carry in us the image of God. We did not evolve by chance from some primordial ooze over eons of time. We were handmade by God Himself. "The LORD God formed the man from the dust of the ground and breathed into his nostrils the breath of life, and the man became a living being.... Then the LORD God made a woman from the rib he had taken out of the man, and he brought her to the man" (2:7, 22 NIV).

God showed His love for humans by creating them in His image and likeness. And then God placed them in a perfect, sinless garden paradise to work, play, and enjoy each other as husband and wife, and to experience a personal relationship with God Himself (3:8). Not only did God create Adam and Eve in His own image, He created them with the ability to enjoy a personal, intimate relationship with each other and Himself. He also created them with the freedom to choose whether to return His love or reject it. God didn't make robots. He didn't use His power to manipulate and coerce. He created humans with a free will to choose life or death, relationship or isolation, good or evil.

God told Adam, "You are free to eat from any tree in the garden; but you must not eat from the tree of the knowledge of good and evil, for when you eat of it you will surely die" (2:16–17 NIV). Sadly, Adam and Eve used their freedom to rebel against God, and this rebellion severed their relationship with God. But it did not extinguish His love for them. This takes us to the next dimension of God's love.

Dimension 2: Redemption. God knew that Adam and Eve ate from the Tree of the Knowledge of Good and Evil. He knew that they had rebelled against His will and that He must enforce the penalty of death. But even in executing judgment, God showed His undying love for humans as He provided a substitute to make atonement for their sin. "The LORD God made garments of skin for Adam and his wife and clothed them" (3:21 NIV). This was the first sacrifice for sin, and it paints a beautiful picture of the Lord Jesus Christ who would one day come to earth as God's Son and shed His blood on a cross to pay the price for the sin of the world. "God made him who had no sin to be sin for us, so that in him we might become the righteousness of God" (2 Cor. 5:21 NIV).

The sacrifice for sin in the garden was a forecast of redemption, the complete payment for sin that Jesus would provide through His substitutionary death on the cross. God's love for humanity is revealed as He steps in to pay the price for sin. That doesn't mean that sin is without its consequences. Adam and Eve would physically die one day as a result of their sin. Adam would toil in working the ground as the effects of the curse infected nature, and Eve would experience pain both in childbirth and in relationship with her husband. Sin is not without its consequences, but it is also not without God's willingness to forgive and restore fallen, rebellious, sinful humans back into relationship with Him.

Knowing that our sin is forgiven as we accept Jesus' payment on the cross assures us of an eternal home in heaven. This takes us to the third dimension of God's love.

Dimension 3: Preparation. When Jesus left the earth, He promised His followers: "In my Father's house are many rooms.… I am going there to prepare a place for you. And if I go and prepare a place for you, I will come back and take you to be with me that you also may be where I am" (John 14:2–3 NIV). Since the day that Jesus left the earth over two thousand years ago, He has been in heaven with the Father preparing a place for us, His children. Even though today we toil, even though we experience suffering and death in this life, there is a new life coming and a new order of things that will once again place us into the very presence of God. "Now the dwelling of God is with men, and he will live with them. They will be his people, and God himself will be with them and be their God. He will wipe every tear from their eyes. There will be no more death or mourning or crying or pain, for the old order of things has passed away" (Rev. 21:3–4 NIV).

Don't let the troubles of this life get you down, because there is so much life and love ahead. Instead, immerse yourself in the knowledge of God's love, which serves as the beginning point of all that we know about God. And walk in the freedom of your new life in Christ, living each day with one eye on eternity.

***

Dr. Wiersbe's commentaries have been a source of guidance and strength to me over the many years that I have been a pastor. His unique style is not overly academic, but theologically sound. He explains the deep truths of Scripture in a way that everyone can understand and apply. Whether you're a Bible scholar or a brand-new believer in Christ, you will benefit, as I have, from Warren's insights. With your Bible in one hand and Dr. Wiersbe's commentary in the other, you will be able to accurately unpack the deep truths of God's Word and learn how to apply them to your life.

Drink deeply, my friend, of the truths of God's Word, for in them you will find Jesus Christ, and there is freedom, peace, assurance, and joy.

—Ken Baugh
Pastor of Coast Hills Community Church
Aliso Viejo, California

A Word from the Author

Whether you're learning to use a computer, drive a car, or climb a mountain, you have to start with the basics. As gifted as he was, even Mozart had to master the musical scales; and Shakespeare had to learn the English alphabet before he could write his great plays.

It's hard to believe, but the most brilliant scientist got his or her start in chemistry 101 or physics 101.

During a halftime pep talk to his discouraged team, Coach Vince Lombardi held up a pigskin and said, "This is a football." Their performance had been so dismal that he had to take them back to square one. He knew what all competent people have to know: If you want to succeed, you have to know and master the basics.

Basics are those fundamental truths that are the foundation for the decisions we make, the values we cherish, and the goals we try to reach. If you're wondering why there's so much confusion and destruction in today's world, one reason is because people are ignoring or rejecting the basics. But that's like going on a voyage without a compass or radar, or trying to perform brain surgery without lights.

The book of Genesis is the "book of basics" because it's the "book of beginnings" in the Bible.[1] To know Genesis is to know the fundamental truths—the basics—about God, the world, yourself and other people, law, sin, salvation, marriage, faith, and spiritual fulfillment. Inspired by the Spirit of God, Moses[2] wrote Genesis and told us where we came from, why we're here, and what God expects us to do. Moses also explained how the Jewish nation began, the people through whom God would reveal Himself to the world, write the Bible, and ultimately give us our Savior, the Lord Jesus Christ.

Genesis is the foundational book of the Bible, and the rest of Scripture is built on what Moses wrote. Genesis is quoted or referred to more than two hundred times in the New Testament, which means it's important for the New Testament Christian to understand its message.

As I read book catalogs and scan the shelves in bookstores, I'm fascinated to see the large number of books that have been published on Genesis, written by secular authors as well as by writers of the Judeo-Christian tradition. People are discovering in the ancient book of Genesis the basic truths we need to understand and apply in our fast-paced, social-networking world.

Genesis is God's invitation to you and me to *Be Basic*.

—Warren W. Wiersbe

A Suggested Outline of the Book of Genesis

Theme: Beginnings

Key verse: "In the beginning God ..." (Genesis 1:1)

I. God Creates the Universe (Genesis 1)

II. Adam and Eve (Genesis 2—5)
   A. The garden (Genesis 2)
   B. The fall (Genesis 3)
   C. The consequences of the fall (Genesis 4—5)

III. Noah and His Family (Genesis 6:1—11:9)
   A. The flood (Genesis 6—7)
   B. The new earth (Genesis 8)
   C. The covenant (Genesis 9)
   D. The nations (Genesis 10)
   E. The tower of Babel (Genesis 11:1–9)

IV. Abraham and Sarah (Genesis 11:10—25:11)
   The beginning of the Hebrew nation

V. Isaac and Rebekah (Genesis 25:12—28:22)

VI. Jacob and His Family (Genesis 29:1—38:30)
   The building of the Hebrew nation

VII. Joseph and His Ministry (Genesis 39:1—50:26)
   The protecting of the Hebrew nation

Chapter One

BC: Before Creation

(Genesis 1:1)

I n spite of its name "Genesis," which means "beginning," and in spite of its position as the first book in the Bible, the book of Genesis isn't the beginning of everything. Genesis 1:1 reminds us, "In the beginning God." So, before we study the basics that are laid down in Genesis 1—11, let's acquaint ourselves with what God did before what's recorded in Genesis. After that, we'll examine what He did that's recorded in Genesis, and finally, what occurred after Genesis. This will give us the kind of broad overview we need to study the rest of God's revelation in the Bible.

Before Genesis: Redemption Planned

What was happening before God spoke the universe into existence? That may seem like an impractical hypothetical question, like "How many angels can stand on the point of a pin?" but it isn't.[1] After all, God doesn't act arbitrarily, and the fact that He created something suggests that He must have had some magnificent purposes in mind. What, then, was the situation before Genesis 1:1, and what does it teach us about God and ourselves?

God existed in sublime glory. God is eternal; He has neither beginning nor ending. Therefore, He is totally self-sufficient and needs nothing more than Himself in order to exist or to act. "God has a voluntary relation to everything He has made," wrote A. W. Tozer, "but He has no necessary relation to anything outside of Himself."[2] God needs nothing, neither the material universe nor the human race, and yet He created both.

If you want something to boggle your mind, meditate on the concept of the eternal, that which has neither beginning nor ending. As creatures of time, you and I can easily focus on the transient things around us, but it's difficult if not impossible to conceive of that which is eternal.[3] Contemplating the nature and character of the triune God who always was, always is, and always will be, and who never changes, is a task that overwhelms us. "In the beginning God."

Moses wrote, "Before the mountains were born or you brought forth the earth and the world, from everlasting to everlasting you are God" (Ps. 90:2 NIV). Frederick Faber expressed it like this:

> Timeless, spaceless, single, lonely,[4]
> Yet sublimely Three,
> Thou art grandly, always, only
> God in unity![5]

"Process theology," an old heresy in modern dress, affirms a "limited god" who is in the process of becoming a "greater" god. But if God is God, as we understand the word, then He is eternal and needs nothing; and He is all-knowing, all-powerful, and everywhere present. In order to have a "limited god," you must first redefine the very word "God," because by definition God cannot be limited.

Furthermore, if God is limited and "getting greater," then what power is making Him greater? That power would be greater than "God" and therefore be God! And wouldn't that give us two gods instead of one?[6] But the God of the Bible is eternal and had no beginning. He is infinite and knows no limitations in either time or space. He is perfect and cannot "improve," and is immutable and cannot change.

The God that Abraham worshipped is the eternal God (Gen. 21:33), and Moses told the Israelites, "The eternal God is your refuge, and underneath are the everlasting arms" (Deut. 33:27 NIV). Habakkuk said that God was "from everlasting" (Hab. 1:12; see 3:6), and Paul called Him "the everlasting [eternal] God" (Rom. 16:26; see 1 Tim. 1:17).

The divine Trinity was in loving communion. "In the beginning God" would be a startling statement to a citizen of Ur of the Chaldees where Abraham came from, because the Chaldeans and all their neighbors worshipped a galaxy of greater and lesser gods and goddesses. But the God of Genesis is the only true God and has no "rival gods" to contend with, such as you read about in the myths and fables from the ancient world. (See Ex. 15:1; 20:3; Deut. 6:4; 1 Kings 8:60; 2 Kings 19:15; Ps. 18:31.)

This one true God exists as three Persons: God the Father and God the Son and God the Holy Spirit. (See Matt. 3:16–17; 28:18–20;[7] John 3:34–35; 14:15–17; Acts 2:32–33, 38–39; 10:36–38; 1 Cor. 12:1–6; 2 Cor. 13:14; Eph. 1:3–14; 4:1–6; 2 Thess. 2:13–14; Titus 3:4–6; 1 Peter 1:1–2.) This doesn't mean that one God manifests Himself in three different forms, or that there are three gods; it means that one God exists in three Persons who are equal in their attributes and yet individual and distinct in their offices and ministries. As the Nicene Creed (AD 325) states it, "We believe in one God … And in one Lord Jesus Christ, the Son of God, begotten of the Father, light of light, very God of very God, begotten, not made, being of one substance with the Father … And in the Holy Ghost."

I once heard a minister open a worship service by praying, "Father, thank You for dying for us on the cross." But it was God the Son, not God the Father, who died for sinners on the cross, and it is God the Holy Spirit who convicts lost sinners and brings them to repentance and salvation. To scramble and confuse the Persons of the divine Godhead is to change what is taught in Scripture, and this is a dangerous thing to do.

The doctrine of the Trinity wasn't clearly revealed in the Old Testament, because the emphasis in the Old Testament is that the God of Israel is one God, uncreated and unique, the only true God. Worshipping the false gods of their neighbors was the great temptation and repeated sin of Israel, so Moses and the prophets hammered away on the unity and uniqueness of Israel's God. Even today, the faithful Jewish worshipper recites "The Shema" each day: "Hear [*shema*], O Israel: the Lord our God, the Lord is one! You shall love the Lord your God with all your heart, with all your soul, and with all your strength" (Deut. 6:4–5 NKJV). The God revealed in Scripture has no peers and no rivals.

But the Old Testament does give glimpses and hints of the wonderful truth of the Trinity, a truth that would later be clearly revealed in the New Testament by Christ and the apostles. The "let us" statements in Genesis (Gen. 1:26; 3:22; 11:7; see also Isa. 6:8) suggest that the Persons of the Godhead worked together in conference, and the many instances when "the angel of the Lord" appeared on the scene indicate the presence of the Son of God. (See Gen. 16:7–11; 21:17; 22:11, 15; 24:7, 40; 31:11; 32:24–30; Ex. 3:1–4 with Acts 7:30–34; Ex. 14:19; 23:20–26; 32:33—33:17; Josh. 5:13ff.; Judg. 2:1–5 and 6:11ff.)

Messiah (God the Son) speaks about Himself, the Spirit, and the Lord (Father) in Isaiah 48:16–17 and 61:1–3, and Psalm 2:7 states that Jehovah has a son. Jesus applied verse 7 to Himself when He challenged His enemies who did not accept Him as the Son of God (Matt. 22:41–46; see also Ps. 110:1). In Genesis 1:2 and 6:3, the Spirit of God is distinguished from the Lord (Father), and this same distinction is found in Numbers 27:18; Psalm 51:11; Isaiah 40:13; 48:16; and Haggai 2:4–5.

Though the word "trinity" is nowhere used in the Bible, the doctrine is certainly there, hidden in the Old Testament and revealed in the New Testament. Does this profound and mysterious doctrine have any practical meaning for the believer today? Yes, because the three Persons of the

Godhead are all involved in planning and executing the divine will for the universe, including the plan of salvation.

The divine Trinity planned redemption. The wonderful plan of redemption wasn't a divine afterthought, for God's people were chosen in Christ "before the foundation of the world" (Eph. 1:4; see Rev. 17:8) and given by the Father to the Son both to belong to His kingdom (Matt. 25:34) and to share His glory (John 17:2, 6, 9, 11–12, 24). The sacrificial death of the Son wasn't an accident, it was an appointment (Acts 2:23; 4:27–28), for He was "slain from the foundation of the world" (Rev. 13:8).

In the counsels of eternity, the Godhead determined to create a world that would include humans made in the image of God. The Father was involved in creation (Gen. 1:1; 2 Kings 19:15; Acts 4:24), but so were the Son (John 1:1–3, 10; Col. 1:16; Heb. 1:2) and the Holy Spirit (Gen. 1:2; Ps. 104:30). God didn't create a world because He needed anything but that He might share His love with creatures who, unlike the angels, are made in the image of God and can respond willingly to His love.

The Godhead determined that the Son would come to earth and die for the sins of the world, and Jesus came to do the Father's will (John 10:17–18; Heb. 10:7). The words Jesus spoke were from the Father (John 14:24), and the works He did were commissioned by the Father (John 5:17–21, 36; Acts 2:22) and empowered by the Spirit (Acts 10:38). The Son glorifies the Father (John 14:13; 17:1, 4) and the Spirit glorifies the Son (John 16:13–14). The Persons of the Holy Trinity work together to accomplish the divine will.

According to Ephesians 1:3–14, the plan of salvation is Trinitarian: We are chosen by the Father (vv. 3–6), purchased by the Son (vv. 7–12), and sealed by the Spirit (vv. 13–14), and all of this is to the praise of God's glory (vv. 6, 12, 14).[8] The Father has given authority to the Son to give eternal life to those He has given to the Son (John 17:1–3). All of this was planned before there was ever a world!

It's important to see that all three Persons in the Godhead share in the salvation of lost sinners. As far as God the Father is concerned, I was saved when He graciously chose me in Christ before the foundation of the world, but I knew nothing about divine election until after I was converted.[9] As far as God the Son is concerned, I was saved when He died for me on the cross, and I knew that great truth from the earliest days of my life. But as far as God the Holy Spirit is concerned, I was saved in May 1945 when the Spirit of God convicted me and I trusted Jesus Christ. Then what God had planned from eternity all fell into place in my life.

Spiritual birth is something like human birth: You experience it but it takes time to understand it! After all, I wouldn't know my own birthdate if somebody hadn't told me. It's after we've been born into God's family that the wonder of it all is revealed to us from the Word, and then we want to share it with others.

When you seek to fathom the depths of the divine eternal counsels, you will be overwhelmed. But don't be discouraged, for over the centuries, good and godly scholars have disagreed in their speculations and conclusions. One of my seminary professors used to remind us, "Try to explain these things and you may lose your mind; but try to explain them away, and you will lose your soul."

Moses said it best: "The secret things belong to the Lord our God, but those things which are revealed belong to us and to our children forever, that we may do all the words of this law" (Deut. 29:29 NKJV). The important thing is not knowing all that God knows but doing all God tells us to do. "For we know in part" (1 Cor. 13:9).

GENESIS: REDEMPTION PROMISED

When He wrote the Bible, God didn't give us a ponderous theology book divided into sections labeled *God, Creation, Man, Sin,* and so forth. Instead, He gave us a story, a narrative that begins in eternity past and ends in eternity future. It's a story about God and His dealings with all kinds of people and how they responded to His Word. As we read these narratives, we learn a great deal about God, ourselves, and our world, and we discover that our own personal story is found somewhere in the pages of Scripture. If you read long enough and honestly enough, you will meet yourself in the Bible.

In our versions of the Bible, there are fifty chapters in Genesis, but the original Hebrew text isn't divided. After describing the creation (1:1—2:3), Moses listed eleven "generations" that comprise the Genesis narrative: the heavens and the earth (2:4—4:26); Adam (5:1—6:8); Noah (6:9—9:29); Noah's sons, Shem, Ham, and Japheth (10:1—11:9), with an emphasis on Shem, father of the Semites (11:10–26); Terah, father of Abraham (11:27—25:11); Ishmael (25:12–18); Isaac (25:19—35:29); Esau (36:1–8), who is also Edom (36:9—37:1); and Jacob (37:2—50:13). These are the individuals presented in Genesis.

The first eleven chapters of Genesis deal with *humanity in general* and focus on four great events: creation (1—2), the fall of man and its consequences (3—5), the flood (6—9), and the rebellion at Babel (10—11). The rest of Genesis focuses on *Israel in particular* (12—50) and recounts the lives of four great men: Abraham (12:1—25:18), Isaac (25:19—27:46), Jacob (28—36), and Joseph (37—50).[10] We call these men the "patriarchs" because they were the founding fathers of the Hebrew nation.

As you study Genesis, keep in mind that Moses didn't write a detailed history of each person or event. He recorded only those things that helped him achieve his purpose, which was to explain the origin of things, especially the origin of the Jewish nation. Genesis 1—11 is a record of failure, but with the call of Abraham, God made a new beginning. Man's sin had brought God's curse (3:14, 17; 4:11), but God's gracious covenant with Abraham brought blessing to the whole world (12:1–3).

You will also notice in the Genesis record that when man does his worst and reaches his lowest, God gives him a new beginning. Dr. G. Campbell Morgan said that the cycle in Genesis is "generation, degeneration, and regeneration."[11] Cain killed Abel, but God gave Seth to continue the godly line. The earth became violent and wicked, so God wiped out humanity but chose Noah and his family to carry on His work. Out of pagan Ur of the Chaldees, God called Abraham and Sarah and gave them a son, Isaac, and the future of God's plan of salvation rested with that son. Isaac and Rebekah had two sons, Esau and Jacob, but God rejected Esau and chose Jacob to build the twelve tribes of Israel and inherit the covenant blessings.

In other words, from beginning to end, Genesis is the story of God's sovereign will and electing grace. This doesn't suggest that the persons in the story were mere robots, because they made mistakes and even tried to thwart God's plans. But whenever people resisted God's rule, He overruled and accomplished His divine purposes anyway. "The counsel of the Lord stands forever, the plans of His heart to all generations" (Ps. 33:11 NKJV).

What begins in Genesis is developed throughout the Bible and then finds its fulfillment in the book of Revelation, as you can see from this summary:

Genesis	Revelation
The first heaven and earth	The new heaven and earth
The first garden; the Tree of Life guarded	The "garden city" and the Tree of Life available
The first marriage	The last marriage, the marriage of the Lamb
Satan tempts Eve to sin	Satan thrown into the lake of fire

Death enters the scene	"No more death"
Babylon built	Babylon destroyed
The Redeemer promised	The Redeemer reigns

There are many more comparisons and contrasts between these two books, but this gives you some idea of how important Genesis is to an understanding of God's program and the rest of Scripture.

AFTER GENESIS: REDEMPTION ACCOMPLISHED

God revealed His great plan of salvation gradually. First, He gave a promise (Gen. 3:15), the first salvation promise found in the Bible. It's the promise of a Redeemer who would be born of a woman, defeat Satan, and bring salvation to mankind. The promised Savior would be a man and not an angel and would save humans and not fallen angels (Heb. 2:5–18).

Where would this promised Redeemer come from? Genesis 12:1–3 answers that question: The Redeemer will be a Jew, from the people of Abraham. Through a miracle of God, Abraham and Sarah had Isaac, and Isaac was the father of Jacob. But Jacob had twelve sons who founded the twelve tribes of Israel. Which of them would give the world the Savior? Genesis 49:10 tells us: The Redeemer will come from the tribe of Judah.

The book of Exodus tells how God built the great Hebrew nation as they suffered in the land of Egypt and then delivered them by His great power. They should have claimed their inheritance in Canaan, but in unbelief they disobeyed God and ended up wandering forty years in the wilderness (Num. 13—14). Joshua led the new generation into the land and there established the nation.

After the tragic era of the rule of the judges and the reign of Saul, recorded in Judges and 1 Samuel, God anointed David as king and revealed that the promised Redeemer would come from David's family (2 Sam. 7). He would not only be "the son of David," but he would also be born in Bethlehem, the city of David (Mic. 5:2). Through Isaiah the prophet, God announced that the Redeemer would be born of a virgin in a miraculous way (Isa. 7:14; see Luke 1:26–38).

Of course, throughout the Old Testament ages, Satan did all he could to thwart the plans of God. Cain belonged to the Devil (1 John 3:12) and killed his brother Abel, but God gave Seth to continue the godly line (Gen. 4:25–26). During the flood, God preserved Noah and his family, and from the family of Shem, Abraham was born, the father of the Hebrew nation.

On at least four occasions, the godly line was threatened with extinction. Twice Abraham lied about Sarah his wife and she was taken by pagan rulers (Gen. 12:10–20; 20:1ff.), and his son Isaac committed the same sin and jeopardized his wife Rebekah (26:6–16). During the dark days of the later Hebrew monarchy, the wicked Queen Mother Athaliah had all the royal sons slain, but one little prince, Joash, was rescued to continue the Davidic line (2 Kings 11).

How did it all end? "But when the fullness of the time had come, God sent forth His Son, born of a woman, born under the law, to redeem those who were under the law" (Gal. 4:4–5 NKJV). The angel announced to the shepherds, "For unto you is born this day in the city of David a Saviour, which is Christ the Lord" (Luke 2:11).

The promise had been fulfilled! And it all started in Genesis!

Now let's join Moses and read his magnificent inspired record of the creation of the heaven, the earth, and human life.

QUESTIONS FOR PERSONAL REFLECTION
OR GROUP DISCUSSION

1. In what area of your life have you ever had to go "back to the basics"?

2. What, in your opinion, are the "basics" for life?

3. How does being creatures of time affect our view of God and of ourselves?

4. Who is the "Trinity"? How would you explain the Trinity to someone new in the faith?

5. Even though the doctrine of the Trinity is not clearly revealed in the Old Testament, what hints of the Trinity does the Old Testament give us?

6. How is it important for us to see the Trinity as a loving communion?

7. What truths have you only gradually come to understand since the time of your new birth?

8. Why do you think God chose to reveal Himself in stories, rather than just statements of fact?

9. What do the first eleven chapters of Genesis focus on?

10. Why is it helpful to know that what begins in Genesis is fulfilled in Revelation?

11. Genesis reveals God's sovereignty. How is God sovereignly at work in your life?

Chapter Two

WHEN GOD SPEAKS, SOMETHING HAPPENS

(Genesis 1)

S ome people call the president of the United States "the most powerful leader in the world," but more than one former president would disagree. Ex-presidents have confessed that their executive orders weren't always obeyed and that there wasn't much they could do about it.

For example, during President Nixon's first term in office, he ordered the removal of some ugly temporary buildings on the mall, eyesores that had been there since the World War I era, but it took many months before the order was obeyed. When journalists began writing about "the imperial presidency," Nixon called the whole idea "ludicrous."[1] Presidents may speak and sign official orders, but that's no guarantee that anything will happen.

However, when God speaks, *something happens!* "For He spoke, and it was done; He commanded, and it stood fast" (Ps. 33:9 NKJV). When you consider the acts of God recorded in Genesis 1, you can't help but bow in reverent worship, for His creative acts reveal a God of power and wisdom whose word carries authority.

GOD CREATES (1:1–2)

Three books of the Bible open with "beginnings": Genesis 1:1; Mark 1:1; and John 1:1. Each of these beginnings is important. "In the beginning was the Word" (John 1:1) takes us into eternity past when Jesus Christ, the living Word of God, existed as the eternal Son of God. John wasn't suggesting that Jesus had a beginning. Jesus Christ is the eternal Son of God who existed before all things because He made all things (John 1:3; Col. 1:16–17; Heb. 1:2). Therefore, John's "beginning" antedates Genesis 1:1.[2]

The gospel of Mark opens with, "The beginning of the gospel of Jesus Christ, the Son of God." The message of the gospel didn't start with the ministry of John the Baptist, because the good news of God's grace was announced in Genesis 3:15. As Hebrews 11 bears witness, God's promise was believed by people throughout Old Testament history, and those who believed were saved. (See Gal. 3:1–9 and Rom. 4.) The ministry of John the Baptist, the forerunner of Jesus, was the beginning of the *proclamation* of the message concerning Jesus Christ of Nazareth (see Acts 1:21–22 and 10:37).

"In the beginning God created the heaven and the earth" (Gen. 1:1) refers to the dateless past when God brought the universe into existence out of nothing (Ps. 33:6; Rom. 4:17; Heb. 1:3).[3] Genesis 1:1–2 is the *declaration* that God created the universe; the detailed *explanation* of the six days of God's creative work is given in the rest of the chapter.

Thirty–two times in this chapter, this creative God is called Elohim, a Hebrew word that emphasizes His majesty and power. (The covenant name "Jehovah" ["Lord"] appears for the first time in Gen. 2:4.) Elohim is a plural noun that is consistently used in connection with singular verbs and adjectives. (Hebrew tenses are singular, dual, or plural.) Some think that this plural form is what grammarians call the "plural of majesty," or it might also be a hint that God exists in three persons. In Scripture, creation is attributed to the Father (Acts 4:24) and to the Son (John 1:1–3) and to the Holy Spirit (Ps. 104:30).

Elohim reveals His power by creating everything by merely speaking the word. Matter is not eternal; it began when God spoke everything into existence (Eph. 3:9; Col. 1:16; Rev. 4:11). Scripture doesn't reveal why God chose to start His creative work with a chaotic mass that was dark, formless, and empty,[4] but the Holy Spirit, brooding over the waters,[5] would bring order out of chaos and beauty and fullness out of emptiness.[6] He can still do that today with the lives of all who will yield to Him.

The nations that surrounded the people of Israel had ancient traditions that "explained" the origin of the universe and humankind. These myths involved monsters that battled in deep oceans and gods who fought battles to bring the universe into being. But the simple account in Genesis presents us with one God who alone created all things and is still in control of His creation. Had the Jewish people paid close attention to what Moses wrote, they would never have worshipped the idols of their pagan neighbors.

GOD FORMS (1:3–13)

There's a pattern to God's activities during the creation week: first He *formed* and then He *filled*. He made three spheres of activity: the heavens, the landmasses, and the waters; and then He filled them with appropriate forms of life.

Day one (vv. 3–5). God commanded the light to shine and then separated the light from the darkness. But how could there be light when the light-bearers aren't mentioned until the fourth day (vv. 14–19)? Since we aren't told that this light came from any of the luminaries God created, it probably came from God Himself who is light (John 1:5) and wears light as a garment (Ps. 104:2; Hab. 3:3–4). The eternal city will enjoy endless light without the help of the sun or moon (Rev. 22:5), so why couldn't there be light at the beginning of time before the luminaries were made?[7]

Life as we know it could not exist without the light of the sun. Paul saw in this creative act the work of God in the new creation, the salvation of the lost. "For it is the God who commanded light to shine out of darkness, who has shone in our hearts to give the light of the knowledge of the glory of God in the face of Jesus Christ" (2 Cor. 4:6 NKJV). "In him [Jesus] was life; and the life was the light of men" (John 1:4).

In verse 4, God deemed the light "good." In Scripture, light is associated with Christ (8:12), the Word of God (Ps. 119:105, 130), God's people (Matt. 5:14–16; Eph. 5:8), and God's blessing (Prov. 4:18), while darkness is associated with Satan (Eph. 6:12), sin (Matt. 6:22–23; John 3:19–21), death (Job 3:4–6, 9), spiritual ignorance (John 1:5), and divine judgment (Matt. 8:12). This explains why God separated the light from the darkness, for the two have nothing in common. God's people are to "walk in the light" (1 John 1:5–10), for "what communion hath light with darkness?" (2 Cor. 6:14–16; see Eph. 5:1–14).

From the very first day of creation, God established the principle of separation. Not only did He separate the light from the darkness (Gen. 1:4) and the day from the night (v. 14), but later He also separated the waters above from the waters beneath (vv. 6–8), and the land from the waters (vv. 9–10). Through Moses, God commanded the people of Israel to remain separated from the nations around them (Ex. 34:10–17; Deut. 7:1–11), and when they violated this commandment, they suffered. God's people today need to be careful in their walk (Ps. 1:1) and not be defiled by the world (Rom. 12:1–2; James 1:6–8; 4:4; 1 John 2:15–17).

Since God is the Creator, He has the right to call things whatever He pleases, and thus we have "day" and "night." The word "day" can refer to the portion of time when the sun is visible as well as to the whole period of twenty-four hours composed of "evening and morning" (Gen. 1:5).[8] Sometimes biblical writers used "day" to describe a longer period of time in which God accomplishes some special purpose, such as "the day of the Lord" (Isa. 2:12) or "the day of judgment" (Matt. 10:15).

When we speak about spiritual things, it's important that we use God's dictionary as well as His vocabulary. Words carry meanings and giving the wrong meaning to a word could lead to serious trouble. It would be fatal to a patient if a physician confused "arsenic" with "aspirin," so medical people are very careful to use accurate terminology. The "Christian vocabulary" is even more important because eternal death could be the consequence of confusion. The Bible explains and illustrates words like sin, grace, forgiveness, justification, and faith, and to change their meanings is to replace God's truth with lies. "Woe unto them that call evil good, and good evil; that put darkness for light, and light for darkness; that put bitter for sweet, and sweet for bitter" (Isa. 5:20).

Day two (vv. 6–8). God put an expanse between the upper waters and the lower waters and made "heaven," what we know as "the sky." It seems that these waters were a vaporous "blanket" that covered the original creative mass. When separated from the landmass, the lower waters eventually became the ocean and the seas, and the upper waters played a part in the flood during Noah's day (Gen. 7:11–12; 9:11–15).

The word translated "firmament" (expanse) means "to beat out." In Scripture, the sky is sometimes referred to as a dome or a covering; however, Scripture nowhere supports the pagan mythological notion that the sky is some kind of solid covering. The luminaries were set in this expanse (1:14–17) and that's where the fowl flew (v. 20).

Day three (vv. 9–13). God gathered the waters and caused the dry land to appear, thus making "earth" and "seas." Israel's pagan neighbors believed all kinds of myths about the heavens, the earth, and the seas; but Moses made it clear that Elohim, the one true God, was Lord of them all. For the second time, God said that what He had done was "good" (v. 10; "light" being the first, v. 4). God's creation is still good, even though it travails because of sin (Rom. 8:20–22) and has been ravaged and exploited by sinful people.

God also caused plant life to appear on the earth: the grasses, the seed-producing herbs, and the fruit-bearing trees. God decreed that each would reproduce "after its kind," which helps to make possible order in nature. God has set reproductive limits for both plants and animals (Gen. 1:21) because He is the Lord of Creation. There's no suggestion here of any kind of "evolution." God was preparing the earth for a habitation for humans and for animals, and the plants would help to provide their food. A third time, God said that His work was good (v. 12).

GOD FILLS (1:14–27; 2:7)

God has now created three special "spaces": the land, the seas, and the expanse of the sky. During the next three creative days, He will fill these spaces.

Day four (vv. 14–19). Into the expanse of the sky God placed the heavenly bodies and assigned them their work: to divide the day and night and to provide "signs" to mark off days, years, and seasons. Light had already appeared on the first day, but now it was concentrated in these heavenly bodies.

Because of their religious observances, the Jews needed to know the times and the seasons, when the Sabbath arrived and ended, when it was a new month, and when it was time to celebrate their annual feasts (Lev. 23). Before the invention of the clock and the compass, the activities of human life were closely linked to nature's cycles, and navigators depended on the stars to direct them. Israel would need the help of the heavenly bodies to direct their activities, and God would occasionally use signs in the heavens to speak to His people on earth.[9]

Israel was commanded not to imitate their pagan neighbors by worshipping the heavenly bodies (Ex. 20:1–6; Deut. 4:15–19; 17:2–7). They were to worship the true God who created the "heavenly host," the army of heaven that did His bidding. However, the Jews didn't obey God's commandment (Jer. 8:2; 19:13; Ezek. 8:16–18; Zeph. 1:4–6) and suffered greatly for their sins.

The ancient peoples were fascinated by the moon and stars and the movements of the sun and planets, and it was but a short step from admiration to worship. "If the stars should appear one night in a thousand years," wrote Ralph Waldo Emerson, "how would men believe and adore; and preserve for many generations the remembrance of the city of God which had been shown …"[10]

Day five (vv. 20–23). God had created the sky and the waters, and now He filled them abundantly with living creatures. He made birds to fly in the sky and aquatic creatures to frolic in the seas. "O Lord, how manifold are Your works! In wisdom You have made them all. The earth is full of Your possessions—This great and wide sea, in which are innumerable teeming things, living things both small and great" (Ps. 104:24–25 NKJV).

A new element is added to God's work on this day: He not only called His work "good," but He blessed the creatures He had made. This is the first time the word "bless" is used in the Bible. God's blessing enabled the creatures and the fowl to reproduce abundantly and enjoy all that He had made for them. God would also bless the first man and woman (Gen. 1:28; 5:2), the Sabbath day (2:3), and Noah and his family (9:1). After creation, perhaps the most important occasion for God's blessing was when He gave His gracious covenant to Abraham and his descendants (12:1–3). That blessing has reached down to God's people today (Gal. 3:1–9).

Day six (vv. 24–31; 2:7). God had formed the sky and filled it with heavenly luminaries and flying birds. He had formed the seas and filled the waters with various aquatic creatures. Creation reaches its climax when on the sixth day He filled the land with animal life and then created the first man who, with his wife, would have dominion over the earth and its creatures.

Like the first man, the animals were formed out of the dust of the ground (2:7), which explains why the bodies of both humans and animals go back to the dust after death (Eccl. 3:19–20). However, humans and animals are different. No matter how intelligent some animals may appear to be, or how much they are taught, animals are not endowed with the "image of God" as are humans.[11]

The creation of the first man is seen as a very special occasion, for there's a "consultation" prior to the event. "Let us make man in our image" sounds like the conclusion of a divine deliberation among the persons of the Godhead.[12] God couldn't have been talking with the angels about His plans because angels weren't made in God's image ("our image"), and angels had nothing to do with the creation of Adam.

"And the Lord God formed man of the dust of the ground, and breathed into his nostrils the breath of life; and man became a living soul" (Gen. 2:7). The verb "formed" suggests the potter making a work of art in his skilled hands. The human body is indeed a work of art, an amazingly complex organism that only the wisdom of God could design and the power of God create.

The physical matter for Adam's body came from the ground, for the name "Adam" means "taken out of the ground," but the life Adam possessed came from God. Of course, God is spirit and doesn't have lungs for breathing. This statement is what theologians call an "anthropomorphism," the using of a human characteristic to explain a divine work or attribute.[13]

Several important facts must be noted about the origin of humans. First, *we were created by God.* We are not the products of some galactic accident nor are we the occupants of the top rung of an evolutionary ladder. God made us, which means we are creatures and wholly dependent on Him. "For in him we live, and move, and have our being" (Acts 17:28). Luke 3:38 calls Adam "the son of God."

Second, *we were created in God's image* (Gen. 1:26–27). Unlike the angels and the animals, humans can have a very special relationship with God. He not only gave us personality—minds to think with, emotions to feel with, and wills for making decisions—but He also gave us an inner spiritual nature that enables us to know Him and worship Him. The image of God in men and women has been marred by sin (Eph. 4:18–19), but through faith in Christ and submission to the work of the Holy Spirit, believers can have the divine nature renewed within them (2 Peter 1:4; Eph. 4:20–24; Col. 3:9–10; Rom. 12:2; 2 Cor. 3:18). One day when we see Jesus, all of God's children will share in the glorious image of Christ (1 John 3:1–3; Rom. 8:29; 1 Cor. 15:49).

Third, *we were created to have dominion over the earth* (Gen. 1:26, 28).[14] Adam and Eve were the first regents over God's creation (Ps. 8:6–8). "The heaven, even the heavens, are the Lord's; but the earth He has given to the children of men" (Ps. 115:16 NKJV). But when Adam believed Satan's lie and ate of the forbidden fruit, he lost his kingship, and now sin and death reign over the earth (Rom. 5:12–21).

When Jesus Christ, the last Adam (1 Cor. 15:45), came to earth, He exercised the dominion that the first Adam had lost. He demonstrated that He had authority over the fish (Luke 5:1–7; John 21:1–6; Matt. 17:24–27), the fowl (26:69–75), and the animals (Mark 1:13; 11:3–7). When He died on the cross, He conquered sin and death, so that now grace can reign (Rom. 5:21) and God's people can "reign in life" through Jesus Christ (v. 17). One day, when He returns, Jesus will restore to His own the dominion that was lost because of Adam (Heb. 2:5ff.).

Both Adam and the animal creation were vegetarians until after the flood (Gen. 1:29–30; 9:1–4). Isaiah 11:7 indicates that the carnivorous beasts will return to this diet when Jesus Christ returns and establishes His kingdom on earth.

Fourth, *this wonderful Creator deserves our worship, praise, and obedience.* When God surveyed His creation, He saw that it was "very good" (Gen. 1:31). Contrary to what some religions and philosophies teach, creation is not evil and it isn't a sin to enjoy the good gifts God shares with us (1 Tim. 6:17). David surveyed God's creation and asked, "What is man that You are mindful of him, and the son of man that You visit him?" (Ps. 8:4 NKJV).

The earth is but a tiny planet orbiting in a vast galaxy, and yet "the earth is the Lord's" (24:1). It's the one planet He has chosen to visit and to redeem!

The heavenly creatures before God's throne praise Him for His creation, and so should we. "Thou art worthy, O Lord, to receive glory and honor and power: for thou hast created all things, and for thy pleasure they are and were created" (Rev. 4:11). When we bow at meals to thank Him for the food He provides, when we see the sunshine and the rain provided at no expense to us, and when we watch the progress of the seasons, we should lift our hearts to praise the Creator for His faithfulness and generosity.

Finally, *we must be good stewards of creation.* This means we should respect our fellow human beings who are also made in the image of God (Gen. 9:6). It means appreciating the gifts we have in creation and not wasting or exploiting them. We'll look into these matters in greater detail in further studies, but it's worth noting that we can't honor the God of creation if we dishonor His creation. We must accept creation as a gift, guard it as a precious treasure, and invest it for the glory of God. Isaac Watts said it beautifully in his hymn "I Sing the Mighty Power of God":

> I sing the goodness of the Lord,
> that filled the earth with food;
> He formed the creatures with His word,
> and then pronounced them good.
> Lord, how Thy wonders are displayed,
> where e'er I turn my eye;
> If I survey the ground I tread,
> or gaze upon the sky.

"The Lord is good to all: and his tender mercies are over all his works" (Ps. 145:9).

QUESTIONS FOR PERSONAL REFLECTION
OR GROUP DISCUSSION

1. God's Word carries absolute authority: "For He spoke, and it was done" (Ps. 33:9 NKJV). How does this affect your relationship with God?

2. At creation, God spoke powerful words. What powerful words has God spoken on your behalf?

3. In what sense do our words have power?

4. What is the significance of the word *day*? What difference does it make if "day" means twenty-four hours or "a period of time"?

5. When have you heard people use God's vocabulary (words) without using His dictionary (true meanings)?

6. What do you believe about creation and evolution? What questions do you still have? Where can you find the answers?

7. The admiration of creation soon turned to worship. Where do you observe this happening today?

8. What is the essential difference between animals and humans? How do you know this?

9. According to Wiersbe, what important facts should we remember about the origin of humans? Why are these important?

10. This week, how can you express your praise to God because of His magnificent creation?

Chapter Three

FIRST THINGS FIRST

(Genesis 2)

I f you could have been present to witness any event in Bible history, which event would you choose?

I once asked that question of several well-known Christian leaders, and the answers were varied: the crucifixion of Christ, the resurrection of Christ, the flood, Israel crossing the Red Sea, and even David slaying Goliath. But one of them said, "I would like to have been present when God finished His creation. It must have been an awesome sight!"

Some scientists claim that if we could travel out into space fast enough and far enough, we could "catch up" with the light beams from the past and watch history unfold before our eyes. Perhaps the Lord will let us do that when we get to heaven. I hope so, because I would like to see the extraordinary events Moses described in Genesis 1 and 2.

Genesis 2 introduces us to a series of "firsts" that are important to us if we want to build our lives according to the basics God has put into His universe.

THE FIRST SABBATH (2:1–3)

The word "Sabbath" isn't found in this paragraph, but Moses is writing about the Sabbath, the seventh day of the week. The phrase "seventh day" is mentioned three times in verses 2–3. "Sabbath" comes from a Hebrew word *shabbat* that means "to cease working, to rest" and is related to the Hebrew word for "seven."[1] We need to consider three different Sabbaths found in the Bible.

The personal Sabbath of the Lord God (vv. 1–4). This first Sabbath didn't take place because God was tired from all His creative work, because God doesn't get weary (Isa. 40:28). God set apart the seventh day because His work of creation was finished and He was pleased and satisfied with what He had created. "And God saw everything that he had made, and, behold, it was very good" (Gen. 1:31).

Three things are distinctive about this seventh day of the creation week. First, there's no mention of "evening and morning," suggesting that God's Sabbath rest would have no end. Unfortunately, man's sin interrupted God's rest, and God had to search for Adam and Eve and deal with them (3:8–9, and see John 5:9, 17). Second, there's no record that He blessed any of the other six days, but God did bless the seventh day (Gen. 2:3). In blessing it, He made it a blessing. Third, after blessing the seventh day, God sanctified it (v. 3), which means He set it apart for His own special purposes.[2]

Jehovah is the God of time as well as the Lord of eternity. It was He who created time and established the rotation of the planets and their orbits around the sun. It was He who marked out the seven-day week and set aside one day for Himself. Every living thing that God has created lives a day at a time except humans made in God's image! People rush around in the frantic "rat race" of life, always planning to rest but never seeming to fulfill their plan.

It has been said that most people in our world are being "crucified between two thieves": the regrets of yesterday and the worries about tomorrow. That's why they can't enjoy today. Relying on modern means of transportation and communication, we try to live two or three days at a time, only to run headlong against the creation cycle of the universe, and the results are painful and often disastrous.

A famous Chinese scholar came to America to lecture and during the course of his tour was met at a busy metropolitan railway station by his university host. "If we run quickly, we can catch the next train and save ourselves three minutes," said the host. The scholar quietly asked, "And what significant thing shall we do with the three minutes that we save by running?" A good question that could not be answered. Henry David Thoreau wrote in *Walden* over a century ago, "The mass of men lead lives of quiet desperation." I wonder what he'd say if he saw the frantic people running up and down escalators in our airline terminals!

God had done many wonderful things during the six days of creation, but the climax of the creation week was God's "rest" after His work. As we shall see, God has sanctified work as well as rest, but it's rest that seems to be the greatest need in people's hearts today. Augustine was correct when he wrote, "Thou hast made us for Thyself, and our hearts are restless until they rest in Thee."

The national Sabbath of Israel. There's no mention of the Sabbath in Scripture until Exodus 16:23 when God gave the regulations to Israel about gathering the daily manna. From the way this commandment is worded, it suggests that the Jews already knew the importance of the Sabbath and were observing it as a day of rest. In giving the Sabbath to Israel, the Lord related this special day to other events in sacred history.

To begin with, when God gave Israel the law at Mount Sinai, the Sabbath was connected with creation (20:8–11). God was the generous Giver of all that they needed, and they must acknowledge Him by worshipping the Creator and not the creation. They were not to imitate the pagan nations around them (Rom. 1:18ff.). Moses even mentioned the weekly rest needed by servants and farm animals (Ex. 23:12), so keeping the Sabbath was a humanitarian act as well as a religious duty. The Lord commanded His people to observe every seventh year as a Sabbatical Year and every fiftieth year as a Year of Jubilee. This would permit the land to enjoy its Sabbaths and be renewed (Lev. 25).

The Sabbath was not only connected with creation, but at the close of the giving of the law, it was vested with special significance *as a sign between Israel and Jehovah* (Ex. 31:12–17; Neh. 9:13–15). "Surely My Sabbaths you shall keep, for it is a sign between Me and you throughout your generations, that you may know that I am the Lord who sanctifies you" (Ex. 31:13 NKJV). There's no evidence that God ever required any other nation to observe the Sabbath, because the Jews alone were the chosen people of God.

There's a third connection between the Sabbath and the Jews. When Moses rehearsed the law for the new generation about to enter Canaan, he connected the Sabbath Day *with their deliverance from Egypt* (Deut. 5:12–15). The weekly Sabbath and the annual Passover feast would both remind Israel of God's mercy and power in freeing the nation from bondage. Furthermore, this weekly day of rest would also be a foretaste of the rest they would enjoy in the Promised Land (Deut. 3:20; 12:10; 25:19; Josh. 22:4). God had brought them out of Egypt that He might bring them into the Promised Land to claim their inheritance (Deut. 4:37–38). In the book of Hebrews, this concept of a "promised rest" is applied to believers today.

The nation of Israel eventually declined spiritually and didn't observe God's laws, including the Sabbath law, and they were ultimately punished for their disobedience (2 Chron. 36:14–21; Ezek. 20:1ff.; Isa. 58:13–14; Jer. 17:19–27). The northern kingdom of Israel was swallowed up by Assyria, and the Southern Kingdom of Judah was taken into captivity by Babylon.

By the time of the ministry of Jesus, the scribes and Pharisees had added their traditions to God's Word and turned the law in general and the Sabbath in particular into religious bondage. The few prohibitions found in Moses (Ex. 16:29; 35:2–3; Num. 15:32–36) were expanded into numerous regulations. Jesus, however, rejected their traditions and even performed miracles on the Sabbath! He said, "The sabbath was made for man, and not man for the sabbath" (Mark 2:27).

The spiritual Sabbath of the Christian believer (Heb. 4:1–11).
Hebrews 4 brings together God's creation rest (v. 4) and Israel's Canaan
rest (v. 8) to teach us about the spiritual rest that believers have in Christ
(vv. 9–11). When you trust Jesus Christ, you enter the "new creation"
(2 Cor. 5:17) and into His spiritual rest (Matt. 11:28–30). You also enter
into the spiritual inheritance He gives all who trust Him (Acts 20:32; Eph.
1:18; Col. 1:12). Believers are not under bondage to keep the law (Gal. 5:1)
because the Holy Spirit fulfills the righteousness of the law in us as we yield
to Him (Rom. 8:1–3).

The first Christian believers met daily for worship and fellowship (Acts
2:46), but they also gathered together on the first day of the week, the day
of Christ's resurrection from the dead (John 20:19, 26; Acts 20:7; 1 Cor.
16:2). The first day was known as "the Lord's day" (Rev. 1:10); and to make
the Lord's Day into a "Christian Sabbath" is to confuse what these two
days stand for in God's plan of salvation.

The seventh day of the week, the Jewish Sabbath, symbolizes the old
creation and the covenant of law: first you work, then you rest. The first day
of the week, the Lord's day, symbolizes the new creation and the covenant
of grace: first you believe in Christ and find rest, and then you work (Eph.
2:8–10). In the new creation, God's Spirit enables us to make the entire
week an experience of worship, praise, and service to the glory of God.

The Jewish Sabbath law was fulfilled by Christ on the cross and is no
longer binding on God's people (Gal. 4:1–11; Col. 2:16–17). However,
some believers may choose to honor the Sabbath day "as unto the Lord,"
and Christians are not to judge or condemn one another in this matter.
When good and godly people disagree on matters of conscience, they
must practice love and mutual acceptance and grant one another liberty
(Rom. 14:1—15:7). "So let no one judge you in food or in drink [the
dietary laws], or regarding a festival or a new moon [the Jewish feasts] or
sabbaths" (Col. 2:16 NKJV).

The First Home (2:4–14)

Some Old Testament scholars have claimed that this section of Genesis 2 is a second account of creation written by a different author whose message conflicts with what's found in chapter 1. That theory isn't widely promoted today; for in these verses, Moses tells the same creation story but adds details that we need to know in order to understand events that happen later. Genesis 2:4 is the first of eleven "generation" statements that mark the progress of the story Moses wrote in the book of Genesis. (See chapter 1, section 2.)

Adam the worker. Looking back to the third day (1:9–13), Moses told how God had brought forth vegetation and provided a "mist" to water the plants. You won't encounter rain in Genesis until the time of the flood. It's interesting that God needed someone to till the earth and help produce the food needed. Humans are stewards of God's creation blessings and should use His gifts as He commands. God and man work together, for God put Adam into the garden to do His work in tilling the soil and caring for it (2:15).

A retired man living in a city got tired of seeing an ugly vacant lot as he took his daily walk, so he asked the owner for permission to plant a garden there. It took days to haul away the accumulated rubbish and even more time to prepare the soil, but the man worked hard. The next year, the lot was aglow with life and beauty, and everyone took notice.

"God has certainly given you a beautiful piece of property," said a visitor as he admired the flowers and the landscaping.

"Yes, He has," the busy gardener replied, "but you should have seen this property when God had it all by Himself!"

The reply was a wise one and not at all irreverent. The same God who ordains the end—a beautiful garden—also ordains the means to the end—someone to do the work. After all, "faith without works is dead" (James 2:26), and no amount of prayer or Bible study can take the place of a gardener plowing the soil, sowing the seed, watering plants, and pulling weeds. "For we are laborers together with God" (1 Cor. 3:9).

Work isn't a curse; it's an opportunity to use our abilities and opportunities in cooperating with God and being faithful stewards of His creation. After man sinned, work became toil (Gen. 3:17–19), but that wasn't God's original intention. We all have different abilities and opportunities, and we must discover what God wants us to do with our lives in this world, for the good of others and the glory of God. Someday, we want to be able to stand before God and say with Jesus, "I have glorified You on the earth. I have finished the work which You have given Me to do" (John 17:4 NKJV).

Adam the tenant. God planted His garden "eastward in Eden" (Gen. 2:8). "Eden" means either "delight" or "place of much water" and suggests that this garden was a paradise from the hand of God. Bible history begins with a beautiful garden in which man sinned, but the story ends with a glorious "garden city" (Rev. 21—22) in which there will be no sin. What brought about the change? A third garden, Gethsemane, where Jesus surrendered to the Father's will and then went forth to die on a cross for the sins of the world.

We have no information about the Pishon River or the Gihon River, and though the Tigris (Hiddekel) and Euphrates are familiar to us, we still don't have enough data to determine the exact location of the garden of Eden. The location of the land of Havilah is also uncertain; some place it in Armenia, others in Mesopotamia. The *King James Version* has identified the land of Cush as Ethiopia, but this interpretation isn't generally accepted today. Fortunately, it isn't necessary to master ancient geography in order to understand the spiritual lessons of these early chapters in Genesis.

In this beautiful garden, God provided both bounty and beauty; Adam and Eve had food to eat and God's lovely handiwork to enjoy. As yet, sin hadn't entered the garden; so their happiness wasn't marred.

THE FIRST COVENANT (2:16–17)

A covenant is a binding arrangement between two or more parties that governs their relationship.[3] The word *command* is introduced at this point because it's God who makes the terms of the agreement. God is the Creator and man is the creature, a "royal tenant" in God's wonderful world, so God has the right to tell the man what he can and cannot do. God didn't ask for Adam's advice; He simply gave him His commandment.

God had given great honor and privilege to Adam in making him His vice-regent on the earth (1:28), but with privilege always comes responsibility. The same divine Word that brought the universe into being also expresses God's love and will to Adam and Eve and their descendants (Ps. 33:11). Obedience to this Word would keep them in the sphere of God's fellowship and approval. All God's commands are good commands and bring good things to those who obey them (Ps. 119:39; Prov. 6:20–23). "And his commands are not burdensome" (1 John 5:3 NIV).

God placed two special trees in the middle of the garden: the Tree of Life and the Tree of the Knowledge of Good and Evil (Gen. 2:9, 17; 3:3, 22, 24). Eating from the Tree of Life would confer immortality (v. 22). Eating from the second tree would confer an experiential knowledge of good and evil, but it would also bring death (2:17).[4] Since they had never experienced evil, Adam and Eve were like innocent children (Deut. 1:39; Isa. 7:15–16). When they disobeyed God, they became like Him in being able to discriminate between good and evil, but they became unlike Him in that they lost their sinlessness and eventually died.

But why did God have to test Adam and Eve? There may be many answers to that question, but one thing is sure: God wanted humans to love and obey Him freely and willingly and not because they were programmed like robots who had to obey. In one sense, God "took a risk" when He made Adam and Eve in His own image and gave them the privilege of choice, but this is the way He ordained for them to learn about freedom and obedience. It's one of the basic truths of life that obedience brings blessing and disobedience brings judgment.

THE FIRST MARRIAGE (2:19–25)

At the close of the sixth day of creation, God had surveyed everything He had made and pronounced it "very good" (1:31). But now God says that there's something in His wonderful world that is not good: The man is alone. In fact, in the Hebrew text, the phrase "not good" is at the beginning of the Lord's statement in 2:18.

What was "not good" about man's solitude? After all, Adam could fellowship with God, enjoy the beauty of the garden and eat of its fruits, accomplish his daily work, and even play with the animals. What more could he want? God knew what Adam needed: "a helper suitable for him" (v. 18 NIV). There was no such helper among the animals, so God made the first woman and presented her to the man as his wife, companion, and helper. She was God's special love gift to Adam (3:12).

The dignity of woman (vv. 18–22). The woman was by no means a "lesser creature." The same God who made Adam also made Eve and created her in His own image (1:27). Both Adam and Eve exercised dominion over creation (v. 29). Adam was made from the dust, but Eve was made from Adam's side, bone of his bone and flesh of his flesh (2:23).

The plain fact is that Adam needed Eve. Not a single animal God had created could do for Adam what Eve could do. She was a helper "meet [suitable] for him." When God paraded the animals before Adam for him to name them, they doubtless came before him in pairs, each with its mate, and perhaps Adam wondered, "Why don't I have a mate?"

Though Eve was made to be a "suitable [face-to-face] helper" for Adam, she wasn't made to be a slave. The noted Bible commentator Matthew Henry wrote: "She was not made out of his head to rule over him, nor out of his feet to be trampled upon by him, but out of his side to be equal with him, under his arm to be protected, and near his heart to be beloved." Paul wrote that "the woman is the glory of man" (1 Cor. 11:7 NIV), for if man is the head (1 Cor. 11:1–16; Eph. 5:22–33), then woman is the crown that honors the head.

The sanctity of marriage (vv. 23–24).[5] God's pattern for marriage wasn't devised by Adam; as the traditional marriage ceremony states it, "Marriage was born in the loving heart of God for the blessing and benefit of mankind." No matter what the courts may decree, or society may permit, when it comes to marriage, God had the first word and He will have the last word (Heb. 13:4; Rev. 22:15). Perhaps the Lord looks down on many unbiblical marriages today and says, "From the beginning it was not so" (Matt. 19:8). His original plan was that one man and one woman be one flesh for one lifetime.

God had at least four purposes in mind when He performed the first marriage in the garden of Eden. First, He wanted suitable companionship for Adam, so He gave him a wife. He gave Adam a person and not an animal, someone who was his equal and therefore could understand him and help him. Martin Luther called marriage "a school for character," and it is. As two people live together in holy matrimony, the experience either brings out the best in them or the worst in them. It's an opportunity to exercise faith, hope, and love and to mature in sacrifice and service to one another for God's glory.

Second, marriage provides the God-given right to enjoy sex and have children. The Lord commanded them to "be fruitful, and multiply, and replenish the earth" (Gen. 1:28). This doesn't imply that sexual love is only for procreation, because many people marry who are beyond the time of bearing children, but the bearing of children is an important part of the marriage union (1 Tim. 5:14).[6]

A third purpose for marriage is to encourage self-control (1 Cor. 7:1–7). "It is better to marry than to burn with passion" (v. 9 NKJV). A marriage that's built only on sexual passion isn't likely to be strong or mature. Sexual love ought to be enriching and not just exciting, and marriage partners need to respect one another and not just use one another. Throughout Scripture, sexual union outside of marriage is condemned and shown to be destructive, and so are the perversions of the sexual union (Rom. 1:24–27). No matter what the judges or the marriage counselors say, "God will judge the adulterer and all the sexually immoral" (Heb. 13:4 NIV).

Finally, marriage is an illustration of the loving and intimate relationship between Christ and His church (Eph. 5:22–33). Paul called this "a great mystery," that is, a profound spiritual truth that was once hidden but is now revealed by the Spirit. Jesus Christ is the Last Adam (1 Cor. 15:45) and therefore a type of the first Adam.

Adam was put to sleep and his side opened that he might have a wife, but Jesus died on a cross and His blood shed that He might have a bride, the church (John 19:33–37). Christ loves the church, cares for it, and seeks to cleanse it and make it more beautiful for His glory. One day Christ will claim His bride and present her in purity and glory in heaven (Jude 24; Rev. 19:1–9).

When Adam saw his bride, he burst into joyful praise (Gen. 2:23), as though he were saying, "At last I have a suitable companion!" (The NIV sets this apart as a poem.) Her identity as "woman" would remind everybody that she was taken out of "man," and the term "man" would always be a part of "woman."[7] She was made from him and for him, and he needed her; therefore, they will always belong to each other and lovingly serve each other.

Adam didn't speak the words recorded in verses 24–25. They are God's reflection on the event and His enunciation of the principle of marital unity declared by Adam. Woman is one with man both in origin (she came from man) and in marriage. In the sexual union and in their children, the man and woman are "one flesh." Marriage is a *civil* relationship, regulated by law, and should be a *spiritual* relationship and a *heart* relationship, governed by the Word of God and motivated by love. But marriage is basically a physical relationship. The man and the woman are not primarily "one spirit" or "one heart," as essential as those things are, but "one flesh." Hence, the importance of "leaving" the former family and "cleaving" to one's mate (Eph. 5:30–31), the forming of a new relationship that must be nurtured and protected.

The phrase "one flesh" implies that anything that breaks the physical bond in marriage can also break the marriage itself. One such thing is death, for when one mate dies, the other mate is free to remarry because the marriage bond has been broken (Rom. 7:1–3; 1 Cor. 7:8–9; 1 Tim. 5:14). In Matthew 19:1–9, Jesus teaches that adultery can also break the marriage bond. Under the Old Testament law, anybody who committed adultery was stoned to death (Deut. 22:22–24; John 8:3–7), thus leaving the innocent mate free to remarry, but this law wasn't given to the New Testament church. It appears that divorce in the New Testament is the equivalent of death in the Old Testament and that the innocent party is free to remarry. However, sins against the marriage bond can be forgiven and couples can exercise forgiveness and make a new beginning in the Lord.

We live in a world created by God, we are creatures made in the image of God, and we enjoy multiplied blessings from the hand of God. How tragic that so many people leave God out of their lives and become confused wanderers in an unfriendly world, when they could be children of God in their Father's world.

QUESTIONS FOR PERSONAL REFLECTION
OR GROUP DISCUSSION

1. How is it significant for us that, after creating the universe, the Lord God blessed and set apart the Sabbath day for rest?

2. When in your life has the following phrase been true: "always planning to rest but never seeming to fulfill their plan"?

3. Are you afflicted by the two thieves Wiersbe mentions: "The regrets of yesterday and the worries about tomorrow"? If so, how?

4. What does this statement by Jesus mean: "The sabbath was made for man, and not man for the sabbath"?

5. What is the difference between the Lord's Day and the Jewish Sabbath?

6. How should Christians view work?

7. What was life like in the garden of Eden?

8. Why did God test Adam and Eve?

9. For what purpose(s) did God create Eve, and indirectly, marriage?

10. What aspects of the way God ordered human life in the beginning do you most need to pay attention to as you seek to set your life in order?

Chapter Four

THIS IS MY FATHER'S WORLD—OR IS IT?

I confess to my shame that during my early years of ministry I avoided having the congregation sing "This Is My Father's World" in our worship services. Except for one line, the song emphasizes the God of nature and not the God of the cross, and I wanted everything in our services to be "evangelical." Furthermore, the language of the song was too sentimental for me, and I wondered what kind of person the composer was. Without even investigating, I concluded that anybody with a name like Maltbie D. Babcock had to be a tubercular recluse who passed away the long hours of each day looking out the window and writing maudlin poetry.

Imagine how shocked and embarrassed I was to discover that Maltbie D. Babcock (1858–1901) was a virile Presbyterian pastor who was an excellent baseball pitcher and a champion swimmer. Most mornings, he went jogging for eight to ten miles! He told people he was going out "to see my Father's world."

Of course, I've matured a bit since those salad days and have repented of my folly. Someday I want to meet Pastor Babcock in heaven and apologize to him. I've come to realize that David was right in praising the

Creator in his psalms, and that the glorified beings in heaven are doing the right thing when they worship God both as Creator (Rev. 4) and Redeemer (Rev. 5), because the two go together. Creation and redemption are part of one great plan, because the redemption wrought by Jesus on the cross will bring freedom to all of nature. One day God's creation will joyfully enter into "the glorious liberty of the children of God" (Rom. 8:21). Hallelujah!

But not everybody agrees with David and Paul and the heavenly worshippers that this is indeed "our Father's world." In his *Prejudices: Third Series,* the American newspaper editor and essayist H. L. Mencken wrote: "The universe is a gigantic flywheel making 10,000 revolutions a minute. Man is a sick fly taking a dizzy ride on it. Religion is the theory that the wheel was designed and set spinning to give him the ride." The British essayist Walter Savage Landor said, "Taken as a whole, the universe is absurd"; and American physicist Steven Weinberg wrote, "The more the universe seems comprehensible, the more it also seems pointless."

Well, take your choice! But be careful, because the choice you make will determine the kind of life you'll live on this earth and your eternal destiny when you leave it. The atheist says that the universe is only an orderly accident. Agnostics admit that they just don't know and aren't too worried. Theists confess that God originally created everything but has long since forsaken what He made. But the Christian believer still sings, "This is my Father's world."

What difference does it make that Christians believe in a Creator who not only made the universe but also presides over it and controls its destiny? If in church we sing "This Is My Father's World," then how should we live in the marketplace and the neighborhood to prove that we really mean it?

WE WILL WORSHIP GOD ALONE

"Let all the earth fear the Lord; let all the people of the world revere him. For he spoke, and it came to be; he commanded, and it stood firm" (Ps. 33:8–9 NIV).

Creation reveals the existence of God, the power of God, and the wisdom of God. That this complex universe should appear by accident out of nothing from a "big bang" is as probable as the works of Shakespeare resulting from an explosion in a printing plant. Only a God of power could create something out of nothing, and only a God of wisdom could make it function as it does. The scientist is only thinking God's thoughts after Him and discovering the laws that God built into His world at creation.

Paul affirmed that creation proves God's "eternal power and Godhead" (Rom. 1:20); and David sang, "The heavens declare the glory of God; and the firmament shows His handiwork" (Ps. 19:1 NKJV). Jesus didn't hesitate to use the word "creation" (Mark 10:6; 13:19), nor did Paul (Rom. 8:1–20, 22) and Peter (2 Peter 3:4).

Romans 1:18–32 explains the devolution of mankind from the knowledge of the true and living God to the worship of false gods and dead idols. Contrary to what some comparative religion scholars teach, mankind didn't begin its religious journey by worshipping the things of nature and then gradually climb upward to worship one God. Actually, mankind began at the top, knowing the true God, but to gratify their passionate appetites, they refused to worship Him and turned instead to idols. "Thus does the world forget You, its Creator," wrote Augustine, "and falls in love with what You have created instead of with You."

When David considered the greatness of the heavens, he had to ask, "What is man that You are mindful of him, and the son of man that You visit him?" (Ps. 8:3–4 NKJV). The prophet Isaiah contemplated the greatness of the Creator and clearly saw the foolishness of idolatry (Isa. 40:12–26; 45:5–18).

Lord, how Thy wonders are displayed,

Where'er I turn my eye:

If I survey the ground I tread,

Or gaze upon the sky!

—Isaac Watts

A tour guide at an atomic laboratory gave his group an opportunity to ask questions, and one visitor asked: "You say that this whole world that seems so solid is nothing but electric particles in motion. If that's true, what holds it all together?" The guide's honest reply was, "We don't know." But Paul answered that question centuries ago: "all things were created … by him [Jesus Christ] and for him. He is before all things, and in him all things hold together" (Col. 1:16–17 NIV). This is the God we worship, and creation joins with us in praising Him (Ps. 19:1–5; 96:10–13; 148:1–13).

We Will Be Good Stewards of His Creation

When God gave the first man and woman dominion over creation (Gen. 1:26–30), He put them and their descendants under obligation to value His gifts and use them carefully for His glory. God created everything for His glory and pleasure (Rev. 4:11) as well as for our enjoyment and use (1 Tim. 6:17; Acts 17:24–28), and we must always see ourselves as stewards in God's world. To destroy creation and waste its bounties is to sin against God.

In this universe, we have God, people, and the things that God made, among them water, land, animal and plant life, air, and vast resources underground. We're commanded to worship God, love people, and use things for the glory of God and the good of others. When this divine order becomes confused, then God's creation suffers. When in our greed we start lusting after things, we soon begin to ignore God, abuse people, and destroy creation. Novelist Alan Paton wrote, "The ground is holy, being even as it came from the Creator. Keep it, guard it, care for it, for it keeps men, guards men, cares for men. Destroy it and man is destroyed."

God wrote into the law of Moses His concern for people, animals, plants, and the land with its resources. The Sabbath day gave rest to both the workers and their animals (Ex. 20:8–11; 23:12), and the Sabbatical Year and Year of Jubilee gave rest to the land (Lev. 25). Because the Jews didn't obey these laws, they went into captivity so that the land could enjoy its Sabbaths and be renewed (2 Chron. 36:14–21).

God gave Israel regulations concerning lost and fallen animals (Deut. 22:1–4), nesting birds (22:6–7), plowing animals (22:10), and newborn animals (Lev. 22:26–28). The psalmist praised God for His constant concern and care for animals and people (Ps. 104:10–30). There's no escaping the fact that God hasn't deserted His creation, but mankind has certainly desecrated and destroyed God's creation. Why? Because people think they own creation. They forget that we're God's tenants and stewards of His gifts.

Ecology experts claim that approximately one hundred species of plants and animals become extinct *every day,* and that the destruction of forests and the pollution of water and air is producing more and more ecological tragedies as time goes on. Yet God *loves* His creation and wants us to use it lovingly. "The Lord is good to all; he has compassion on all he has made.… The Lord is faithful to all his promises and loving toward all he has made … The Lord is righteous in all his ways and loving toward all he has made" (Ps. 145:9, 13, 17 NIV). Dare we exploit and destroy the creation that God loves?

WE WILL TRUST IN GOD'S PROVIDENCE AND NOT WORRY

The agnostic and atheist have every right to worry because (as someone has said) "they have no invisible means of support." To them, the universe is a self-made impersonal machine, not the creation of a wise God and loving Father. But Christian believers see creation as their Father's world. They call the Creator "Father," and they trust Him with their lives, their circumstances, and their future.

Everything in nature praises the Lord and looks to Him for whatever they need. "These all wait for You, that You may give them their food in due season" (Ps. 104:27 NKJV). There's no evidence that robins get ulcers or that rabbits have nervous breakdowns.

> Said the robin to the sparrow,
> "I should really like to know,
> Why those anxious human beings
> Rush around and worry so."
> Said the sparrow to the robin,
> "I do think that it must be
> That they have no Heavenly Father
> Such as cares for you and me."

The universe isn't a vast machine that God created, wound up, and then abandoned. "The earth is the Lord's, and everything in it, the world, and all who live in it" (Ps. 24:1 NIV). "Whatever the Lord pleases He does, in heaven and in earth, in the seas and in all deep places" (Ps. 135:6 NKJV). "In his hand is the life of every creature and the breath of all mankind" (Job 12:10 NIV).

The word "providence" comes from two Latin words that together mean "to see beforehand." No matter what has to be done, the Lord will see to it (Gen. 22:13–14). Planet Earth isn't staggering around in space like a helpless drunk. God has the whole world in His hands and is working out His divine purposes for the good of His people and the glory of His name. It's that assurance that gives His people peace, no matter how difficult the circumstances may be. "The Lord of hosts is with us; the God of Jacob is our refuge.… Be still, and know that I am God" (Ps. 46:7, 10).

In the Sermon on the Mount (Matt. 5—7), Jesus tells us how to cure anxious care. We must put our lives in the hands of the Father and trust Him to guide us and provide for us a day at a time (6:24–34). If we put *things* first in our lives, then we'll worry and fret, but if we put God's kingdom first, He'll meet our needs and give us His peace (v. 33). He is working all things together for good right now (Rom. 8:28), even though we may not see or understand all that He's doing for us.

WE WILL PRAY TO OUR FATHER

If God the Creator and Lord of the universe is our Father, then it's reasonable that we should talk to Him about the things that concern us. "If you then, being evil, know how to give good gifts to your children, how much more will your Father who is in heaven give good things to those who ask Him!" (Matt. 7:11 NKJV).

But if God is sovereign and has a plan for His people and His world, why pray? Isn't praying interfering with God's will? No, it isn't. Prayer is one of the means God has ordained to accomplish His will in this world. It has well been said that the purpose of prayer is not to get our will done in heaven but to get God's will done on earth. "Your will be done on earth as it is in heaven" (6:10 NIV). If we don't ask, we can't receive (Luke 11:9–10; James 4:1–3); and Jesus, by His example, instruction, and promises, encourages us to ask.

We pray to the Father because we know He is the Creator and "Lord of heaven and earth" (Matt. 11:25; Luke 10:21). The great intercessors in the Bible could all say, "My help comes from the LORD, who made heaven and earth" (Ps. 121:2 NKJV). This was true of Abraham (Gen. 14:22), Hezekiah (2 Kings 19:15), the apostles and the early church (Acts 4:24), Paul (Eph. 3:15), and even our Lord Jesus Christ (Luke 10:21). When you focus on the greatness of God, your own problems and burdens will become smaller and lighter.

WE WILL NOT FEAR TO SUFFER FOR HIS SAKE

"So then, those who suffer according to God's will should commit themselves to their faithful Creator and continue to do good" (1 Peter 4:19 NIV). The Greek word translated "commit" is a banking term that means to "deposit for safekeeping" and implies two things: first, that His people are valuable to the Lord, and second, that He is dependable to care for us. "Casting all your care upon Him, for He cares for you" (1 Peter 5:7 NKJV). After all, if the Creator is able to hold His universe together and keep it functioning to accomplish His will, can't He do the same for our lives, our families, and our ministries? The Creator who knows the number and names of all the stars knows who we are and can meet our deepest needs (Ps. 147:3–6).

Peter wrote his letter to believers in the Roman Empire who were about to enter the "fiery furnace" (1 Peter 1:7; 4:12ff.) and be persecuted for their faith. But when His people are in the furnace, the Creator keeps His eye on the clock and His hand on the thermostat. He knows how long and how much, and He is always in control.

> When through fiery trials thy pathway shall lie,
> My grace all-sufficient shall be thy supply;
> The flame shall not hurt thee; I only design
> Thy dross to consume and thy gold to refine.
>
> —JOHN F. WADE

WE WILL LOVE AND SERVE MANKIND

When Paul addressed the Greek philosophers on Mars Hill, he gave them a short course in theology and anthropology (Acts 17:22–34). He told them that God was the Creator and didn't need their man-made temples and idols, because He is Lord of heaven and earth. We can't give God anything because He made everything, and it's He who gives to us "life, and breath, and all things" (Acts 17:25).

Then Paul ventured into dangerous territory and declared that God made all peoples of "one blood" (v. 26), a statement that must have disturbed the proud Greeks. At that time, they considered themselves a superior people and everybody else "barbarians." But Paul knew that all peoples sprang from Adam and that all races and nations are one family before the Creator. In His providence, God has allowed nations to rise and fall and even to move to new territories, but they are all His creatures, made of the dust and sustained by His power.

In the Old Testament law, God commanded the Israelites to show kindness to the strangers and foreigners in their midst (Ex. 23:9; Lev. 19:34; 23:22; Deut. 10:17–19; 26:1–11). Jesus showed mercy to Gentiles as well as to Jews, and He used a Samaritan as an example of a good neighbor (Luke 10:25–37). Some of the Jews in the early church had a problem accepting the Gentiles, but God made it clear that there was no place for prejudice among His people (Acts 10; 11:1–24; 15:1–29; Gal. 3:26–29).

As long as there are needs to be met, we must be neighbors to one another and help one another. It isn't enough to be faithful in our religious duties; we must also be compassionate toward the needy (Isa. 58:6–11; 1 John 3:16–24; James 2:14–17). Even if people aren't professed believers in Christ, they are humans made in the image of God; and we must do what we can for them.

One December day, my wife and I were driving to see her family in Wisconsin, and our car skidded off the road into the ditch. We weren't hurt and the car wasn't damaged, but we didn't know how the two of us could manage to get the car back on the road. A few minutes later, three men driving by saw our plight, stopped the car, and got out to help us. They didn't ask our nationality or our religious convictions; they simply went to work and got our car out of the ditch. We thanked them profusely and they went on their way. What the Scottish poet Robert Burns called "man's inhumanity to man" certainly wasn't evident that day!

The Jewish scholar Abraham Joshua Heschel called race prejudice "the maximum of hatred for the minimum of reason." But if we're all made "of one blood" (Acts 17:26), how can we despise and mistreat one another; for in so doing, we also hurt ourselves.

We Will Read and Study God's Word

"Your hands have made me and fashioned me; give me understanding, that I may learn Your commandments" (Ps. 119:73 NKJV). The hands that wove us in our mother's womb (139:13–16) also wrote the Word to guide us in our daily lives.[1]

When you purchase a new car or a new appliance, you read the instruction manual to make sure you understand how it works. The Bible is the "instruction manual" for life; it tells us where we came from, what we are, and what God expects us to do. The God who made us knows best how we should live, and if we ignore His counsel and warning, we're heading for trouble. To manage our lives without obeying His Word is like flying an airplane without first having read the manual and taken flight instruction: We're heading for a fall!

The Lord has a divine purpose for each of us to fulfill, and we discover that purpose by reading His Word and obeying it. "The Lord will perfect that which concerns me; Your mercy, O Lord, endures forever; do not forsake the works of Your hands" (138:8 NKJV). The Lord wants to guide each of us and enable us to enjoy what He's planned for us, but we have to be willing to cooperate. To ignore the Bible is to abandon the greatest "life manual" ever given to mankind.

"Trust in the Lord with all your heart, and lean not on your own understanding; in all your ways acknowledge Him, and He shall direct your paths" (Prov. 3:5–6 NKJV). Certainly we must use our minds and think things through, but we must not lean on our own reasoning apart from God's Word. Common sense told young David that the giant Goliath was bigger and stronger than he, but faith said that God would defeat the giant (1 Sam. 17). Human reason told the three Hebrew men that the fiery furnace would cremate them, but faith said that God could protect and preserve them (Dan. 3). "So then faith comes by hearing, and hearing by the word of God" (Rom. 10:17 NKJV).

God is the Creator, and He's given His creatures a book that helps them understand who He is, how He works, and what He wants them to do. It's a book of precepts to obey, promises to believe, and principles to understand. It's also a book about real people, some of whom obeyed the Lord and some who didn't, and from the experiences of these people, we can learn a great deal about what to avoid on the path of life.

We should by all means learn all we can, but everything we learn must be tested by the Word of God. American physicist and Nobel Prize recipient Robert A. Millikan said, "I consider an intimate knowledge of the Bible an indispensable qualification of a well-educated man." Yale University professor William Lyon Phelps agreed when he said, "Everyone who has a thorough knowledge of the Bible may truly be called educated … I believe knowledge of the Bible without a college course is more valuable than a college course without the Bible."

If you believe that God is your Creator, and that you're living in His universe, then listen to what He has to say and obey it, for that's the secret of true fulfillment and success (Josh. 1:7–9).

QUESTIONS FOR PERSONAL REFLECTION OR GROUP DISCUSSION

1. If we take seriously the truth that "This is my Father's world," what are the implications for the way we think and live?

2. How does creation reveal God's existence? His power? His wisdom?

3. Why would anyone turn from worshipping the Creator to worshipping the creation?

4. What is behind humans' careless use of natural resources? What can we do about this?

5. When is it difficult for you to trust in the Lord?

6. What is the role of human prayer in the working out of God's sovereign plan?

7. Why might it be disturbing for someone to think that every person is made from "one blood"?

8. Where in your own life or heart do you encounter racial prejudice?

9. What does it mean to "lean not on your own understanding"?

10. Wiersbe says obeying God is the "secret of true fulfillment and success." Why is this the case? Why is it so hard to do?

Chapter Five

PERILS IN PARADISE

(Genesis 3)

If Genesis 3 were not in the Bible, there would be no Bible as we know it. Why? Because the rest of Scripture documents the sad consequences of Adam's sin and explains what God in His grace has done to rescue us. By grasping the basic truths of this important chapter, you can better understand Paul's discussion of justification in Romans 5, his teaching in 1 Timothy 2:8–15 about men and women in the church, and his explanation in 1 Corinthians 15 of the future resurrection.

Adam's disobedience brought sin into the human race, but the Bible gives us no explanation for the existence of Satan and evil before the fall of man. The record in Genesis 3 is not a myth. If the fall of man didn't actually occur, then the Christian faith is built on fables, not fact, and Jesus Christ suffered needlessly on the cross. From Genesis 3 to Revelation 22, the Bible records the conflict between God and Satan, sin and righteousness, and pleads with sinners to repent to trust God.

THE ENEMY (3:1A)[1]

Satan has been caricatured so much by writers, artists, actors, and comedians that most people don't believe the Devil really exists, or if they do believe he exists, they don't take him seriously. For example, the English novelist Samuel Butler wrote, "It must be remembered that we have heard only one side of the case. God has written all the books."[2] And Mark Twain wrote, "We may not pay Satan reverence, for that would be indiscreet, but we can at least respect his talents."[3] A popular television comedian always got laughs when he said, "The devil made me do it!"

Although we don't understand much about his origin,[4] we know that Satan is real, Satan is an enemy, and Satan is dangerous. Here in Genesis 3, Satan is compared to a serpent, an image that's repeated in 2 Corinthians 11:3. In Revelation 12, he's called a dragon, and both names are combined in 20:2. But Satan is not only a serpent who deceives, he's also a roaring lion who devours (1 Peter 5:8). Among his names are "Abaddon" and "Apollyon" which mean "destroyer" (Rev. 9:11); "Satan" which means "adversary"; and "devil" which means "slanderer."

In John 8:44 (NIV), Jesus called Satan a murderer and "the father of lies." He also called him "the evil one" (Matt. 13:19 NIV) and "the prince of this world" (John 12:31). Paul and John also called the Devil "the evil one" (2 Thess. 3:3 NIV; 1 John 3:12 NIV), and Paul said Satan was "the god of this age" (2 Cor. 4:4 NIV), the ruler of the world system (Eph. 2:2), and the leader of demonic forces of evil (Eph. 6:10–12).

In short, Satan is no pushover, and God's people must be careful not to give him a foothold in their lives (Eph. 4:27). That's why we're studying God's Word and seeking to understand the strategy of Satan (2 Cor. 2:11).

THE STRATEGY (3:1b–5)

A temptation is an opportunity to accomplish a good thing in a bad way. It's a good thing to pass a school examination but a bad thing to do it by cheating. It's a good thing to pay your bills but a bad thing to steal the money for the payments. In essence, Satan said to Eve: "I can give you something that you need and want. You can have it now and enjoy it, and best of all, there won't be any painful consequences. What an opportunity!" Note the stages in Satan's tempting of Eve.[5]

Satan disguised himself (v. 1a). Satan isn't an originator; he's a clever imitator who disguises his true character. If necessary, he can even masquerade as an angel of light (2 Cor. 11:14).[6] When he came into the Garden, Satan used the body of a serpent, one of God's creatures that He had pronounced "good" (Gen. 1:31). Eve didn't seem disturbed by the serpent's presence or its speech, so we assume that she saw nothing threatening about the encounter. Perhaps Eve hadn't been introduced to this species and concluded that it had the ability to speak.[7]

Satan still works today as the great impersonator. He has produced a counterfeit righteousness apart from the righteousness that comes only by faith in the Savior (Rom. 9:30–10:13). Satan has false ministers (2 Cor. 11:13–16) who preach a false gospel (Gal. 1:6–10), and he has false brothers (and sisters) who oppose the true gospel (2 Cor. 11:26). The Devil has gathered his counterfeit Christians into false churches that God calls "synagogues of Satan" (Rev. 2:9), and in these assemblies, Satan's "deep secrets" are taught (v. 24 NIV).

Satan questioned God's word (v. 1b). Second Corinthians 11:3 makes it clear that Satan's target was Eve's mind and that his weapon was deception. By questioning what God said, Satan raised doubts in Eve's mind concerning the truthfulness of God's word and the goodness of God's heart. "Do you really mean that you can't eat from *every* tree?" was the import of the subtle question. "If God really loved you, He would be much more generous. He's holding out on you!" Satan wanted Eve to forget that God had told Adam (who had told her) that they could eat freely of the trees of the garden. For their own good, there was a prohibition: They didn't dare eat from the forbidden tree in the middle of the garden (Gen. 2:15–17).

Eve's reply showed that she was following Satan's example and altering the very Word of God. Compare 3:2–3 with 2:16–17 and you'll see that she omitted the word "freely," added the phrase "nor shall you touch it" (NKJV), and failed to say that God "commanded" them to obey. Note too that Eve copied the Devil further when she spoke of "God" (Elohim) and not "the Lord [Jehovah] God," the God of the covenant. Finally, she said "lest you die"—a possibility—instead of "You shall surely die"—an actuality. So, she *took from* God's Word, added to God's Word, and *changed* God's Word, which are serious offenses indeed (Deut. 4:2; 12:32; Prov. 30:6; Rev. 22:19). She was starting to doubt God's goodness and truthfulness.

Satan denied God's Word (v. 4). "You will not surely die" (NIV) is a direct contradiction of God's "You will surely die" (2:17 NIV). But Satan is a liar (John 8:44) and God is the God of truth (Deut. 32:4), and our response to what God says should be, "Therefore all Your precepts concerning all things I consider to be right" (Ps. 119:128 NKJV). At this point, Eve should have reminded herself of God's Word, believed it, left the serpent, and found her husband. It's when we linger at the place of temptation that we get into trouble, especially when we know what we're thinking is contrary to God's truth. God's truth is our shield and buckler (Ps. 91:4; Eph. 6:16), but it protects us only if we take it by faith and use it.

Satan substituted his own lie (v. 5). "You will be like God" (NIV) is a promise that would get anybody's attention.[8] "Glory to man in the highest!" has always been the rallying cry of those who reject the biblical revelation, whether they espouse godless humanism, materialism, or the so-called New Age religion. (Actually, the philosophy of the New Agers isn't new at all. It's as old as Genesis 3!)

Romans 1:18–32 describes how Gentile civilization from the time of Cain rejected the truth of God and turned to foolishness and lies. They "exchanged the truth of God for the lie, and worshipped and served the creature rather than the Creator" (v. 25 NKJV). Speaking about Satan, Jesus said "for he is a liar, and the father of it" (John 8:44). In defiance of God, humans exchanged God's truth for "the lie" (note the singular), and followed Satan who is the father of "it" (note the singular again).

What is "the lie" (singular) that has ruled civilization since the fall of man? It's the belief that men and women can be their own god and live for the creation and not the Creator *and not suffer any consequences.* Believing this, they refuse to submit to God's truth but prefer to believe Satan's lies and follow his diabolical plan for their destruction. They don't realize that Satan is their master (Eph. 2:1–3) and the lake of fire is their destiny (Matt. 7:13–23; Rev. 20:10–15).

When you review the sequence, you can better understand how Satan leads people to the place of disobedience. Once we start to question God's Word, we're prepared to deny His Word and believe Satan's lies. Then it's just a short step to believing Satan's promises and disobeying God's commands. When our Lord was tempted (Matt. 4:1–11), He answered Satan's lies with God's truth and three times affirmed, "It is written!" Satan wants to deceive our minds (2 Cor. 11:3), but we defeat him by using the spiritual weapons God provides (Eph. 6:10–18; 2 Cor. 10:4–5).

THE TRAGEDY (3:6–7)

Humans are so constructed that they must believe something; if they don't believe the truth, then they'll eventually believe lies (2 Thess. 2:10). But if they believe lies, they will have to suffer the consequences that always come when people reject God's truth.

Disobedience (v. 6). First Eve took the fruit and ate it, and then she took some fruit to her husband and he ate it, so that both of them disobeyed the Lord. Eve was deceived, but Adam sinned willfully with his eyes wide open (1 Tim. 2:14). This is why Paul points to Adam, not Eve, as the one who brought sin and death into the human race (Rom. 5:12–21). "For as in Adam all die" (1 Cor. 15:22).

God sees the first Adam as the head of the human race, the old creation. When Adam sinned, we sinned in him and through him suffered the consequences of sin and death. But God sees Jesus Christ as the Head of the Church, the new creation (2 Cor. 5:17), and through His righteous act of obedience in dying on the cross, we have life and righteousness. Yes, sin and death are reigning in this world, but grace and righteousness are also reigning through Christ (Rom. 5:14, 17, 21). Faith in Jesus Christ moves us out of Adam and into Christ, and we are accepted in His righteousness.

Eve sinned because she was attracted to the fruit of the forbidden tree. She was walking by sight and not by faith in God's Word. Genesis 3:6 parallels 1 John 2:16: "good for food"—"the lust of the flesh"; "pleasant to the eyes"—"the lust of the eyes"; "desirable for gaining wisdom" (NIV)—"the pride of life." These are the things that motivate the people of the world today, and when God's people start thinking like the world, they start living like the world.

We know why Eve succumbed to the temptation, but why did Adam willingly sin when he knew it was contrary to God's will? Did he see a change in Eve and realize that his wife wasn't in the same sphere of life as she had been? Did he have to make a choice between obeying God and staying with the wife he undoubtedly loved? These are questions the Bible neither raises nor answers, and it's unwise for us to speculate. Adam made a choice, the wrong choice, and humanity has suffered ever since.

Knowledge (v. 7a). Satan promised that they would "be like God" (NIV) and know good and evil, and his promise was tragically fulfilled. Adam and Eve lost their innocence and for the first time had a personal realization what it meant to sin. It wasn't necessary for their happiness that they have this knowledge, and it would have been far better had they obeyed and grown in their knowledge of God (John 7:17).

In Scripture, shamelessly exposing the naked body is connected with idolatry (Ex. 32:25), drunkenness (Gen. 9:20–23; Hab. 2:15), and demonism (Luke 8:26–39; Acts 19:16). It's a mark of a decadent society on the threshold of destruction when people make a business out of flagrantly exposing naked human bodies to be the objects of sensual pleasure, either in person, in pictures, or in films. Pornography is big business in today's society.

Shame (v. 7b). Realizing their nakedness for the first time (2:25), they quickly made coverings for their bodies. Sin ought to make us ashamed of ourselves. God has given us an inner judge called "conscience" that accuses when we do wrong and approves when we do right (Rom. 2:12–16). A Native American Christian compared conscience to an arrowhead in his heart. "If I do wrong, it turns and hurts me until I make it right. But if I keep on doing wrong, the arrowhead keeps turning and wears down the points, so it doesn't hurt anymore." The Bible calls that a "seared conscience" (1 Tim. 4:2) or an "evil conscience" (Heb. 10:22) that no longer functions properly.

When people are no longer ashamed of their sins, their character is just about gone. "Were they ashamed when they had committed abomination? No! They were not at all ashamed. Nor did they know how to blush" (Jer. 6:15; 8:12 NKJV). "Yet you have the brazen look of a prostitute; you refuse to blush with shame" (Jer. 3:3 NIV). Sins that used to be committed under cloak of darkness are now exhibited openly in movies and on television, and when people protest, they're called "prudes" or "Puritans."

Fear (v. 8). Sin produces both shame and guilt, and both make sinners want to hide. Adam and Eve felt ashamed because of what they were (naked), and they felt guilty because of what they had done (disobey God). Guilt and fear usually go together, which explains why the pair didn't want to enjoy their evening fellowship with the Lord in the garden. Adam admitted, "I was afraid" (v. 10). Trying to hide from the Lord is certainly a futile endeavor (Ps. 139:1–12), and yet guilty sinners still attempt the impossible.

Shame, fear, and guilt so transform the inner person that Adam and Eve could no longer enjoy their beautiful garden home. The trees they had tended and admired, and from which they had eaten, were now only "things" to be used to hide two frightened sinners from the face of God. This wasn't what the trees wanted to do, but they had no choice. Nature is a window through which we see God, but Adam and Eve made it into a locked door to keep God out! One day the Savior would die on a tree so that frightened sinners could come to the Lord and find forgiveness.

THE DISCOVERY (3:9–13)

How God appeared to our first parents when they fellowshipped with Him in the garden isn't explained to us. He probably assumed a temporary body that veiled His glory, as He would do when He visited Abraham many years later (18:1ff.).

Seeking (v. 8). Adam and Eve should have been running to God, confessing their sin, and asking for His forgiveness. But instead, they were hiding from God, and He had to find them. "There is none who understands; there is none who seeks after God" (Rom. 3:11 NKJV). Evangelist Billy Sunday said that sinners can't find God for the same reason criminals can't find policemen: They aren't looking! The Father interrupted His Sabbath rest to go find the man and the woman He had made in His own image.[9] When Jesus ministered on earth, He said, "For the Son of man is come to seek and to save that which was lost" (Luke 19:10). He too interrupted the Sabbath to heal a sick man (John 5:1–16) and a blind man (John 9), and His defense before the bigoted religious leaders was, "My Father is always at his work to this very day, and I, too, am working ... the Son can do nothing by himself; he can do only what he sees his Father doing, because whatever the Father does the Son also does" (5:17, 19 NIV). Today, through the witness of the church, the Holy Spirit is seeking the lost and bringing them to the Savior (16:7–11; Acts 1:8).

Speaking (vv. 9–13). God doesn't ask questions because He needs information. Being God, He knows everything. Rather, He asks questions for our good, to give us the opportunity to face facts, be honest, and confess our sins. However, we must not think of God speaking to Adam and Eve the way a cruel master would speak to a disobedient slave or an angry judge to a convicted criminal. It was more like a brokenhearted father speaking in love to his wayward children.

First, God called to Adam to give him opportunity to answer and come out into the open.[10] That God called him at all was an act of grace, for God could have spoken the word of judgment and justly destroyed Adam and Eve. Another gracious wonder was that Adam could hear God's voice and respond, for his inner nature had been so polluted by sin that he didn't want to face God.

Once Adam and Eve came out of hiding, Adam confessed their shame (they were naked) and their fear (they were guilty). Without saying it openly, Adam was admitting that they had eaten from the forbidden tree. However, when God asked him point-blank if he had eaten of the tree, Adam never said, "Yes, I did!" Instead, he blamed both God and his wife! When God questioned Eve, she blamed the serpent. (She didn't say, "The serpent that You created," but perhaps she thought it.) There were excuses but no confessions.

To quote Billy Sunday again, "An excuse is the skin of a reason stuffed with a lie." Yes, Eve gave Adam the fruit because the serpent deceived her, but that was no reason Adam had to disobey God. When people start making excuses, it's evidence that they don't sense the enormity of their sins or want to confess them and repent. If sinners can find some loophole, they'll run through it as fast as they can!

THE PENALTY (3:14–19)

God's love for sinners in no way eliminates His holy hatred for sin, for while it's true that "God is love" (1 John 4:8, 16), it's also true that "God is light" (1:5). A holy God must deal with sin, for the good of the sinner and for the glory of His name.

The serpent (vv. 14–15). God pronounced sentence first on the serpent and then on the Devil who had used the serpent. It seems that the creature Satan used was originally upright, because God humiliated it by putting it into the dust (Ps. 72:9; Isa. 49:23; Mic. 7:17). While God did curse the serpent and the ground (Gen. 3:17), He never cursed Adam and Eve.

God's words to Satan (v. 15) are called the *protevagelium,* "the first gospel," because this is the first announcement of the coming Redeemer found in the Bible. To God's old covenant people, this verse was a beacon of hope (Gal. 4:1–4); to Satan, it was God's declaration of war, climaxing in his condemnation (Rom. 16:20); and to Eve, it was the assurance that she was forgiven and that God would use a woman to bring the Redeemer into the world (1 Tim. 2:13–15).

The offspring ("seed") of the serpent and of the woman represent Satan's family and God's family. In the parable of the tares (Matt. 13:24–30, 36–43), Jesus states clearly that Satan has "children," people who profess to be true believers but who are actually counterfeits. The parable reveals that wherever God "plants" a true child of the kingdom, Satan comes along and plants a counterfeit. The two grow together and won't be separated until the harvest at the end of the age.

These are people who reject Jesus Christ and confidently depend on their own religious self-righteousness to get them into heaven. The Pharisees were "children of the devil" according to John the Baptist (Matt. 3:7–10) and Jesus (12:34; 23:15, 28, 33; John 8:44). There's no record that Jesus ever called the publicans and sinners "children of the devil"; He reserved that title for the self-righteous Pharisees who crucified Him.

So, throughout history, there has been a conflict between Satan and God, Satan's children and God's children. As we'll discover in our next study, the battle continued with Cain murdering Abel, for Cain was "of that wicked one" (1 John 3:12), that is, a child of the Devil. During Jewish history, the enemies of the true prophets were the false prophets *who spoke in the name of Jehovah.*

Both Jesus and Paul pictured false teachers as pretenders, "wolves in sheep's clothing" (Matt. 7:13–15; Acts 20:28–31). Satan the counterfeiter has always had his children ready to oppose the people of God. At the end of the age, it will culminate in Christ versus Antichrist, Satan's counterfeit masterpiece (2 Thess. 2; Rev. 13).[11] At the cross, Satan "bruised" Christ's heel, but because of His death and resurrection, Christ crushed Satan's head and won a complete victory over him (Eph. 1:17–23; Col. 2:14–15).

The woman (v. 16). God reinforced His word of hope to Eve by assuring her that she would bear children and therefore not immediately die.[12] But the special privilege of woman as the childbearer (and ultimately the one who brings the Redeemer into the world) would involve multiplied pain in pregnancy as well as submission to her husband. This submission isn't identified as part of a curse or as a mandate for husbands to have sovereign power over their wives. The New Testament makes it clear that husbands and wives who love each other and are filled with the Spirit will be mutually submissive (Eph. 5:21ff.; 1 Cor. 7:1–6).

The man (vv. 17–19). Eve would have pain in the labor of childbirth, but Adam would have pain in his daily labor in the field. As he worked to get his food, Adam would encounter obstacles and have to toil and sweat to get a harvest, and this would remind him that his disobedience had affected creation (Rom. 8:18–23). Even more, as he tilled the soil, he would remember that one day he would die and return to the soil from which he had come. Adam the gardener became Adam the toiler.

THE RECOVERY (3:20–24)

For the sake of His own character and law, God must judge sin, but for the sake of His beloved Son, God is willing to forgive sin. Remember, Jesus is the Lamb "slain from the foundation of the world" (Rev. 13:8; see Acts

2:23; 4:27–28), so that God had already made provision for forgiveness and salvation.

A new name (v. 20). Adam believed God's promises (vv. 15–16) and called his wife's name "Eve," which means "living." Faith simply takes God at His Word and acts upon it.

New clothing (v. 21). God's response to Adam and Eve's faith was to remove their flimsy man-made garments and clothe them with acceptable garments that He Himself provided (Isa. 61:10). Innocent animals had to die so that the man and woman might have a new beginning and be back in fellowship with the Lord. It's a picture of what Jesus did for sinners on the cross when He died for a sinful world (2 Cor. 5:21).

A new home (vv. 22–24). If Adam and Eve ate of the Tree of Life, they would live forever on earth as sinners, and their future would be bleak. They must one day die because "the wages of sin is death" (Rom. 6:23). Therefore, the Lord banished the couple from the garden; in fact, Genesis 3:24 says that He "drove" them out. (See 4:14 and 21:10.) God put angelic guards at the entrance of the garden to make sure Adam and Eve didn't try to reenter. The way to "the Tree of Life" would one day be opened by Jesus Christ through His death on the cross (John 14:6; Heb. 10:1–25; Rev. 2:7; 22:1–2, 14, 19).[13]

Daily life would now become a struggle for the man and woman outside the garden as they toiled for their bread and raised their family. They could still have fellowship with God, but they would daily suffer the consequences of their sin, and so would their descendants after them. The law of sin and death would now operate in the human family until the end of time, but the death and resurrection of the Savior would introduce a new law: "For the law of the Spirit of life in Christ Jesus has made me free from the law of sin and death" (Rom. 8:2 NKJV).

QUESTIONS FOR PERSONAL REFLECTION OR GROUP DISCUSSION

1. What is so crucial about the third chapter of Genesis?

2. How convinced of or aware are you of Satan's influence on your daily life? Why is that?

3. In what disguises might we find Satan today?

4. When have you found yourself doubting God's Word? Why do you think that doubt creeps in?

5. What is the overarching lie, according to Wiersbe, that humans have believed since the fall? Why is this lie so fundamental?

6. What are some of the consequences of rejecting God's truth?

7. Why did God ask Adam and Eve questions after their sin?

8. What is the difference between an excuse and a confession?

9. Why do you suppose God chose those specific consequences for Adam and Eve?

10. In what ways are Christians "free from the law of sin and death"?

Chapter Six

IN CENTER STAGE—CAIN

(Genesis 4:1–24)

 All the world's a stage, and all the men and women merely players," wrote Shakespeare. "They have their exits and their entrances, and one man in his time plays many parts."[1]

Remember those familiar words from English Lit 101? Shakespeare was right: We have many roles to play in life as from time to time we relate to various people and confront different circumstances. The important thing is that we let God write the script, choose the cast, and direct the action. If we disregard Him and try to produce the drama ourselves, the story will have a tragic ending.

That's what ruined Cain, the first human baby born on the stage of Planet Earth: He ignored God's script, "did his own thing," and made a mess out of it. Genesis 4 focuses the spotlight on Cain; he's mentioned sixteen times, and seven times Abel is identified as "his [Cain's] brother." As you consider Cain's life and some of the roles he played, you will better understand how important it is for us to know God and do His will.

THE BROTHER (4:1–2A)

God commanded our first parents to "be fruitful, and multiply, and replenish the earth" (1:28), and they obeyed this mandate (5:4). While it's true that the building of a family isn't the only purpose for marriage, and not every marriage is blessed with children, it's also true that children are a precious gift from God (33:5; 48:9; Ps. 127:3) and should be welcomed with joy. The Jewish people in the Old Testament and the Christians in the first century church would be appalled at today's abortion statistics and the philosophies of the people who produce them.

The name "Cain" sounds like the Hebrew word for "acquired." Eve praised God for helping her through her first pregnancy. After all, this was a new experience for her and she had no doctor or obstetric nurse to assist her. Her second pregnancy brought Abel into the world. His name means "breath" and is the word translated "vanity" at least thirty-eight times in Ecclesiastes. Cain's name reminds us that life comes from God, while Abel's name tells us that life is brief.

Genesis is a "family book" and has a good deal to say about brothers. Being the firstborn son, Cain was special, but because of his sin, he lost everything and Seth took his place (Gen. 4:25). Ishmael was Abraham's firstborn, but God bypassed him and chose Isaac. Esau was Isaac's firstborn son, but he was rejected for Jacob, and Jacob's firstborn son Reuben was replaced by Joseph's two sons (49:3–4; 1 Chron. 5:1–2). In fact, God even rearranged the birth order of Joseph's sons (Gen. 48:8–22). Throughout Old Testament history, God's sovereignty is displayed in His choices of those who receive His blessing, for all that we receive is because of God's grace.

Sibling rivalry among brothers is another theme in Genesis. Ishmael persecuted Isaac; Jacob left home so Esau couldn't kill him; and Joseph's brothers intended to kill him but decided to sell him as a slave. When sin entered the human race, it gave us dysfunctional and fractured families, and only the Lord can put families together again.

THE WORKER (4:2B)

As his sons grew older, Adam put them to work in the fields, and it became evident over the years that each boy had his own interests and skills. Cain became a farmer and Abel became a shepherd; the first of many shepherds found in the Bible, including Abraham, Isaac, Jacob and his sons, Moses, and David.

Adam certainly taught his sons why they worked: It was a part of God's creation mandate, and they were colaborers with God (1:26–31). Work isn't a punishment from God because of sin, for Adam had work to do in the garden before he and his wife yielded to Satan's temptation. The biblical approach to work is that we are privileged to cooperate with God by using His creation gifts for the good of people and the glory of God. (See Col. 3:22–23; 1 Thess. 4:11–12; Eccl. 9:10.)

Work in the will of God isn't a curse; it's a blessing. "Six days you shall labor and do all your work" (Ex. 20:9 NKJV) was as much a part of God's law for Israel as His command to rest on the Sabbath Day. The Bible has nothing good to say about idleness or about the idle people who expect others to provide for them (2 Thess. 3:6–15). Before He began His public ministry, Jesus labored as a carpenter (Mark 6:3), and when he wasn't traveling or preaching, the apostle Paul worked as a tentmaker (Acts 18:1–3).

As Christians, we don't work simply to pay our bills and provide for our needs. We work because it's God's ordained way for us to serve Him and others and thereby glorify God in our lives (1 Cor. 10:31). We don't work just to make a living; we work to make a life, to develop our God-given abilities, and seek to increase the quality and quantity of our labor. Martin Luther told the dairymaids that they could milk cows to the glory of God, and Theodore Roosevelt said that "the best prize that life offers is the chance to work hard at work worth doing." Perhaps the boys asked their father why their work was so difficult, and Adam had to explain that God had cursed the ground because of his own disobedience. "In the sweat of your face you shall eat bread" was God's sentence (Gen. 3:17–19 NKJV), and there was no escape. But this question gave Adam the opportunity to remind his sons of God's promise of a Redeemer and a day when creation would be set free from the bondage of sin (v. 15).

THE WORSHIPPER (4:3–7)

Adam and Eve had learned to worship God during those wonderful days in the garden before sin had brought its curse to their lives and to the ground. Certainly they taught their children about the Lord and the importance of worshipping Him. Workers need to be worshippers or they may become idolaters, focusing on the gifts and not the Giver, and forgetting that God gives the power to work and gain wealth (Deut. 8:10–20).

When God clothed Adam and Eve with the skins of animals (Gen. 3:21), perhaps He taught them about sacrifices and the shedding of blood, and they would have passed this truth along to their children. True worship is something we must learn from God Himself, for He alone has the right to lay down the rules for approaching Him and pleasing Him in worship.

God accepted Abel and his sacrifice, and perhaps indicated this by sending fire from heaven to consume the animals (Lev. 9:24; 1 Kings 18:38; 1 Chron. 21:26), but He rejected Cain and his sacrifice. Cain wasn't rejected because of his offering, but his offering was rejected because of Cain: His heart wasn't right with God. It was "by faith" that Abel offered a more acceptable sacrifice than Cain (Heb. 11:4), which means that he had faith in God and was right with God.

In later years, the law of Moses prescribed offerings of grain and fruit (Lev. 2; Deut. 26:1–11), so we have reason to believe that such sacrifices were acceptable from the beginning. But even had Cain brought animal sacrifices and shed their blood, they wouldn't have been accepted by God because of the state of Cain's heart. Abel brought the best that he had and truly sought to please God, but Cain didn't have that attitude of faith. "Behold, to obey is better than sacrifice, and to hearken than the fat of rams" (1 Sam. 15:22; and see Isa. 1:11–13; Hos. 6:6; Mic. 6:6–8; Mark 12:28–34).

The fact that people attend religious meetings and participate in church activities is no proof that they're true believers. It's possible to have "a form of godliness" but never experience its saving power (2 Tim. 3:5). "These people come near to me with their mouth and honor me with their lips, but their hearts are far from me" (Isa. 29:13 NIV; Matt. 15:8). The most costly sacrifices apart from the submission of the heart can never make the worshipper right before God (Ps. 51:16–17). "The way of Cain" (Jude 11) is the way of self-will and unbelief.

When God rejected his offering, Cain became very angry. (The Hebrew word implies that he was "burning with anger.") God spoke to him personally and tried to lead him back to the way of faith, but Cain resisted. It's just like the Lord to give us another opportunity to obey Him, and it's just like stubborn sinners to refuse His gracious help.

The Lord warned Cain that temptation was like a fierce beast crouching at the door of his life, and he had better not open the door. It's dangerous to carry grudges and harbor bitter feelings in our hearts, because all of this can be used by Satan to lead us into temptation and sin. This is what Paul meant when he wrote "neither give place to the devil" (Eph. 4:27). If we aren't careful, we can tempt ourselves and bring about our own ruin.

THE MURDERER (4:8–10)

We can't separate our relationship with God from our relationship with our brothers and sisters. (That includes our natural brothers and sisters as well as our brothers and sisters in the Lord.) An unforgiving spirit, such as possessed Cain, hinders worship and destroys our fellowship with God and God's people (Matt. 5:21–26; 6:14–15). It's better that we interrupt our worship and get right with a brother than to pollute our sacrifice because we have a bad spirit within.

Murder (v. 8). Anger is a powerful emotion that can lead to violence and even murder. Jesus taught that anger in the heart is the moral equivalent of murder with the hands (Matt. 5:21–26). Every year angry drivers cause accidents that kill over thirty thousand people on the U.S. highways, and angry people who have been fired from their jobs have killed hundreds of innocent people. Had Cain heeded God's warning and accepted His gracious invitation (Gen. 4:7), he would never have become a murderer.

How soon after his worship was rejected did Cain entice his brother away from home and kill him? Was it on the same day, or did he brood over the matter a few days? He probably murdered his brother in his heart many times before he actually committed the deed. He was envious of his brother because of his relationship with God (1 John 3:12), and yet Cain was unwilling to get right with God. When we hate others, it's a sign we're not walking in the light (2:9–11) and that we don't have God's love in our hearts (3:10–16).

Lying (vv. 9–10). Cain was a child of the Devil (1 John 3:12),[2] which means he was a murderer and a liar (John 8:44). He lied to his brother when he enticed him to the place where he killed him. He lied to himself in thinking that he could do such an evil deed and get away with it. Cain even tried to lie to God and cover up his wicked deeds![3]

There's a definite parallel between God's dealings with Cain in Genesis 4 and His dealings with Adam and Eve in chapter 3. In both instances, the Lord asked questions, not to get information (for He knows everything) but to give the culprits an opportunity to tell the truth and confess their sins. In both instances, the sinners were evasive and tried to cover up what they had done, but both times God brought their sins out into the light and they had to admit their guilt.

Adam and Eve had run to hide when they heard God's voice (3:8), but God heard Abel's voice crying from the ground and Cain couldn't hide.[4] The shedding of innocent blood pollutes the land (Num. 35:30–34), and that blood cries out for justice (Job 16:18; Isa. 26:21; Rev. 6:9–10).[5] Adam and Eve were expelled from the garden, and Cain became a rejected wanderer of the earth.

The more you think about Cain's sin, the more heinous it becomes. The murder wasn't motivated by sudden passion; it was carefully premeditated. Cain didn't kill a stranger in defense; he murdered his own brother out of envy and hatred. Furthermore, Cain did it after being at the altar to worship God and in spite of God's warning and promise. Finally, once the horrible deed was done, Cain took it all very lightly and tried to lie his way out of it.

THE WANDERER (4:11–15)

A vagabond has no home; a fugitive is running from home; a stranger is away from home; but a pilgrim is heading home. "I have set before you life and death, blessing and cursing: therefore choose life" (Deut. 30:19). Cain made the wrong choice, and instead of being a pilgrim in life, he became a stranger and a fugitive, wandering the land.

God's curse (v. 12). Jehovah had cursed the serpent (3:14) and the ground (v. 17), but He had not cursed Adam and Eve. However, He did curse their son Cain, who was a child of the Devil (the Serpent). Cain had defiled the ground with his brother's blood, and now the ground wouldn't work for him. If Adam toiled and struggled day after day, he would get a harvest (vv. 17–19), but for Cain, there would never be fruit from his labors. So, he couldn't continue as a farmer. All he could do was wander from place to place and eke out a living.

Cain's regrets (vv. 13–14). Cain never repented of his sins; his words reveal only remorse and regret. He didn't say, "My guilt is more than I can bear." He was concerned only with his punishment, not with his character. If he wandered from place to place, he would be in danger, but if he stayed in one place, he would starve. The earth had turned against him, God had turned against him, and people would turn against him.[6] Anybody Cain met would be a relative who might want to avenge Abel's murder. What could he do?

By hating and murdering his brother and refusing to repent, Cain created for himself an intolerable life. He opened the door to temptation (4:7) and closed the door on his family, God, and his future. No matter where he lived or what he did, Cain would always be a restless man for whom there was no remedy.

God's mercy (v. 15). God did a strange thing: He put a mark on Cain that would protect him from the assaults of people who wanted to kill him. We don't know what this mark was or why people would recognize it as God's protective seal, but it worked. This was purely an act of mercy on God's part.

Why would God allow a diabolical murderer like Cain to go free? In His mercy, God doesn't give us what we do deserve, and in His grace, He gives us what we don't deserve. That's the nature of God. God spared Cain's life, *but that wasn't the end of the story.* Eventually Cain died and "after this the judgment" (Heb. 9:27). The entire civilization that he built was destroyed in the flood, and the record of his life is left in Holy Scripture as a warning to anybody who pretends to worship, plays with sin, and doesn't take temptation seriously. "The way of Cain" (Jude 11) is not the narrow way that leads to life (Matt. 7:13–14).

THE BUILDER (4:16–24)

God kept His Word and protected Cain as he wandered. One day he found a place that seemed right for him to settle down, and he decided to build a city. The earth wouldn't yield its strength to Cain's labor as a farmer, but Cain could labor and build *on the earth* and succeed. However, Cain never ceased to be a fugitive, for the name of the land where he settled means "wandering." His citizenship wasn't in heaven (Phil. 3:20–21 NKJV), nor did he have any hope to reach the heavenly city (Heb. 11:9–16). The only heaven Cain knew was his city on earth.[7]

Was Cain a married man before he wandered from Eden, or did he find a wife during his travels? Did he tell her he had murdered his brother? We don't know, but surely he had to explain the mark God had put on him. It was normal for Cain to seek a wife, for he not only wanted to build a city, but he also wanted to build a family. How else could his name be remembered but in his descendants? Cain didn't know that his name and foul deeds would be written in the Word of God for everybody to read.

Cain's wife bore him a son whom he named Enoch, which is related to the Hebrew word for "consecrated." Cain named his city after his son, but we aren't told to whom or to what the city was consecrated. Six generations of Cain's descendants are named (Gen. 4:17–22), some of whom were famous.

Lamech was the first bigamist; he was also a boastful man and a killer. Why or how the young man wounded him, we don't know; but why should a young man be killed because he caused a wound? Lamech's mentioning of Cain's protection (v. 24) indicates that Cain's story was passed from generation to generation. It also suggests that Lamech thought that God's protection extended to him as well. If God would avenge a murderer like Cain, then surely He would avenge Lamech for "protecting himself." Note that Lamech wants God's protection, but he doesn't mention God's name.

The people in the city of Enoch had varied occupations. Some followed Jabal and took care of livestock (v. 20). Others learned from Jabal's brother Jubal and devoted themselves to making and playing musical instruments (v. 21). The followers of Tubal-Cain were metalworkers (v. 22), which suggests the manufacture of farm implements, building tools, and personal weapons. Cain lived in a society that was rich in culture as well as in industry and food production. In the city of Enoch, they had everything but God.

When you put Cain's family tree next to that of Seth (chap. 5), you can't help but notice the similarity in names. You have Enoch and Enosh (v. 6) and Enoch (v. 18), Mehujael and Mahalalel (v. 12), Methushael and Methuselah (v. 21), and Lamech and Lamech (v. 25). Cain's Lamech has three sons (Jabal, Jubal, and Tubal-Cain), and Noah has three sons (Shem, Ham, and Japheth).

What does this similarity in names mean? Perhaps it's God's way of telling us that the godless line of Cain (which is still with us) does its best to imitate the godly line of Seth. After all, Satan is the counterfeiter. He can imitate the names of the true believers, *but he can't produce the believers.* There's an Enoch in both genealogies, but Cain's Enoch didn't walk with God and one day disappear and go to heaven (v. 24)! "What's in a name?" Nothing, if you don't know and belong to the Lord!

But the tragedy is that these two lines—the ungodly line of Cain and the godly line of Seth—came together and merged (6:1–2). The wall of separation came down, and this eventually created the wicked society whose sins brought on the judgment of the flood. Lamech's brand of violence spread (vv. 5, 11–12), and by the time of the flood, only eight people believed God's warning and acted upon it by faith. The rest were destroyed.

Cain's family tree ends with the family of Lamech (4:19–24), an arrogant murderer whose three sons manufactured things for this world. Seth's line ends with Noah ("rest") whose three sons gave the world a new beginning after the flood. The world of that day probably admired Cain's achievements; God wiped them off the face of the earth.

"And the world is passing away, and the lust of it; but he who does the will of God abides forever" (1 John 2:17 NKJV).

QUESTIONS FOR PERSONAL REFLECTION
OR GROUP DISCUSSION

1. What roles in life has God asked you to play?

2. How can you be sure to follow God's script and not write your own?

3. What is the relationship between dysfunctional families and sin?

4. What is the God-given role of work in our lives?

5. If workers are not also worshipping, what might happen?

6. What was the problem with Cain's offering? What does this teach you about your own offerings?

7. Cain felt jealous and bitter toward Abel, with disastrous results. What is the danger of carrying grudges?

8. Why do people lie? Was lying effective for Cain? What would have been a better solution?

9. How does a remorseful person differ from a repentant person?

10. What can we learn from the fact that God put a protective sign on Cain to prevent others from avenging Abel's death?

Chapter Seven

WHEN THE OUTLOOK IS BLEAK, TRY THE UPLOOK

(Genesis 4:25—6:8)

S in had entered the human race, and it didn't take long for the corruption it spawned to spread and defile God's creation. Like a cancerous tumor, evil infected civilization and brought death wherever it went. God's vice-regents on earth, created in God's image, couldn't manage their own lives let alone God's creation, and things began to fall apart.

This section of Genesis covers over fifteen hundred years of human history, years that are overshadowed by sin and sorrow. But when the night is the darkest, the stars shine the brightest, and when the outlook is grim, the uplook is encouraging. Fifteen different people are named in this section, and four of them stand out because they're associated with something special that God did to encourage His people. Those four were Seth, Enosh, Enoch, and Noah.

SETH—A NEW BEGINNING FROM GOD (4:25; 5:1–5)

The only ray of hope in that dark day was God's promise that a Redeemer would one day be born of the woman and conquer the serpent (3:15). But

Abel was dead, so he couldn't beget a child, and Cain, the unbelieving murderer, had wandered off and built a city in the Land of Nod, east of Eden. Would God's promise be fulfilled? How could it be fulfilled?

God is sovereign in all things and His plans aren't frustrated by the foolish and sinful ways of mankind. Because He is the sovereign God, He "works all things according to the counsel of His will" (Eph. 1:11 NKJV). "But our God is in heaven; He does whatever He pleases" (Ps. 115:3 NKJV). The Lord enabled Eve to conceive and bear a son whom she named Seth ("granted") because God had appointed him to replace Abel.

Genesis 5 is the first genealogy in Scripture and introduces "the book of the generations of Adam" (v. 1). Ten generations are listed here, from Adam to Noah, just as ten generations are listed from Shem to Abraham in "the generations of Shem" (11:10–26).[1] Eight times in Genesis 5 you find the melancholy phrase "and he died," for death was now reigning over mankind because of Adam's sin (Rom. 5:12–17, 21). Sin and death still reign today, but through Jesus Christ we can "reign in life" (vv. 17, see 21).

In Bible history, very often the birth of a baby has made the difference between defeat and victory for God's people. During the Jews' difficult years in Egypt, Moses was born and became the liberator of his people (Ex. 2:1–10). When the lamp of prophecy was burning very low, Samuel was born to bring Israel back to God's Word (1 Sam. 1—3), and when the kingdom was disintegrating under Saul, God sent a son to Jesse whom he named David, the man God had chosen to be the next king (Ruth 4:18–22; 1 Sam. 16). At a very low point in Jewish history, by the grace of God, one little boy continued the messianic line from David (2 Kings 11:1–3). In spite of Satan's attacks and the disobedience of His people, God was faithful to work so that His promise of a Redeemer would be fulfilled.

Knowing this should encourage God's people as they see the world turning more and more toward sin and rebellion. God is sovereign and He will accomplish His purposes.

ENOSH—CALLING ON GOD (4:26; 5:6–11)

Seth was 105 years old when his son Enosh was born (5:6). "Enosh" means "man" and comes from a Hebrew word that means "frail, weak." It's the word for man that emphasizes how fragile and weak we really are in ourselves.

A remarkable thing is recorded in connection with the birth of this boy: At that time, people began to gather together to worship God, proclaim His name, and pray.[2] There was a revival of public worship and believing prayer as the descendants of Seth met together in the name of the Lord. While the worldly Cainites were boasting of their strength and valor (4:23–24), the godly Sethites were giving glory to the name of the Lord.

Throughout sacred history, it has been the godly remnant that has kept the work of the Lord going in this world. Time after time, the nation of Israel drifted into idolatry and spiritual lethargy, but a believing remnant was raised up to keep the light burning. These courageous people cried out to God for deliverance, and He heard them and answered their prayers.

After the flood, Noah's small family was the remnant God used to people the earth. The prophet Elijah thought he was alone in serving Jehovah, but 7,000 people in the land remained faithful to the Lord (1 Kings 19:9–18). Whoever wrote Psalm 119 was part of a faithful remnant (v. 63), and the prophets wrote about the believing remnant in their day (Isa. 10:20–23; 37:31–32; Jer. 11:23; Mic. 4:7; Mal. 3:16). Isaiah named one of his sons "a remnant shall return" (Isa. 7:3 NKJV), and a remnant did return to their land after the Babylonian captivity. God used them to rebuild the temple and the city of Jerusalem and to restore the Jewish nation as a political entity.

How many people does God need to get a job done? Ten righteous people in Sodom could have saved the city from destruction (Gen. 18:16ff.), and Jesus said that He was present if only two or three were gathered in His name (Matt. 18:20). Jesus sent the Holy Spirit at Pentecost to empower

120 believers (Acts 1:15—2:4), and Paul evangelized the Roman Empire with a small team of men and women who were wholly devoted to the Lord. God has always looked to the remnant to pray, trust Him, and get the work done.

So, when the work of the Lord looks like it's failing, and you feel like you're the only one left to serve God, remember Enosh and the godly remnant in his day that called on the Lord. "For nothing restrains the Lord from saving by many or by few" (1 Sam. 14:6 NKJV).

ENOCH—WALKING WITH GOD (5:12–27)

People like Kenan, Mahalalel, and Jared may not seem important to God's great story of salvation, but they are important, for they were "living links" in the great generational chain that reached from Seth to the birth of Jesus Christ. God's promise in Genesis 3:15 could never have been fulfilled were it not for the faithfulness of many undistinguished people who to us are only strange names in an ancient genealogy.

When Enoch was sixty-five years old, his wife gave birth to a son whom they named Methuselah ("man of the dart"). This was a turning point in Enoch's life, because he then began to walk with the Lord (5:22, 24; see 6:9). Did the responsibility of raising a son in such a godless world so challenge Enoch that he knew he needed the Lord's help? Or when the baby was born, did God give Enoch insight into the future so that he knew the flood was coming? We don't know, but we do know that the arrival of this baby changed Enoch's life.

The meaning of Methuselah's name isn't significant, but his long life of 969 years is significant. In the year that Methuselah died, the flood came![3] Perhaps the Lord told Enoch this news after the baby was born, and it so gripped his heart that he began to walk with God and do God's will. "Therefore, since all these things will be dissolved, what manner of persons ought you to be in holy conduct and godliness" (2 Peter 3:11 NKJV). The fact that Jesus is coming again to judge the world ought to motivate God's people to lives of holiness and obedient service (1 John 2:28—3:3).

The sobering phrase "and he died" isn't used of Enoch, because Enoch is one of two men in Scripture who never died. Both Enoch and Elijah were taken to heaven alive (2 Kings 2:1–11). Some students see in Enoch's pre-flood "rapture" a picture of the church being taken to heaven before God sends tribulation on the earth (1 Thess. 4:13—5:11).

It was "by faith" that Enoch was taken to heaven (Heb. 11:5). He believed God, walked with God, and went to be with God, which is an example for all of us to follow. Imagine how difficult it must have been to walk with God during those years before the flood, when vice and violence were prevalent and only a remnant of people believed God (Gen. 6:5). But Enoch's life of faith wasn't a private thing, for he boldly announced that God would come to judge the world's sins (Jude 14–15). In his day, the judgment of the flood did come, but the judgment Enoch was announcing will occur when Jesus Christ returns, leading the armies of heaven and condemning Satan and his hosts (Rev. 19:11ff.). Enoch's life and witness remind us that it's possible to be faithful to God in the midst of "a crooked and perverse nation" (Phil. 2:15). No matter how dark the day or how bad the news, we have the promise of our Lord's return to encourage us and motivate us to be godly. One day sin will be judged and God's people will be rewarded for their faithfulness, so we have every reason to be encouraged as we walk with God.

NOAH—REST AND COMFORT FROM GOD (5:28—6:8)

Though they bore the same name, Lamech in the line of Seth was radically different from Lamech in the line of Cain (4:18–24). Seth's Lamech fathered a son, Noah, who walked with God (6:9) and was used of God to save the human race and continue the messianic promise. Cain's Lamech murdered a young man who had wounded him and then boasted to his wives about his evil deed (4:23).

Hope (5:28–32). Lamech's great concern was that mankind find comfort and rest in the midst of a wicked world where it was necessary to toil and sweat just to stay alive. Life was difficult, and the only hope that true believers had was the coming of the promised Redeemer. Lamech named his son Noah, which sounds like the Hebrew word for "comfort." His prayer was that his son would somehow bring to the world the rest and comfort that people so sorely needed. Centuries later, weary people would hear the voice of Jesus say, "Come to Me, all you who labor and are heavy laden, and I will give you rest" (Matt. 11:28 NKJV).

Lamech was 682 years old and Noah 500 years old when Noah's son Japheth was born. The listing in Genesis 5:32 is not the sons' birth order, because Ham was Noah's youngest son (9:20–24) and Japheth his eldest (10:21). The birth order would be Japheth, Shem, and Ham.

Compromise (6:1–7). After chapter 3, Satan isn't mentioned by name in Genesis, but he and his demonic hosts are at work doing their utmost to keep the promised Redeemer from being born. This was Satan's purpose throughout all of Old Testament history. After all, he didn't want to have his head crushed by the Savior (3:15)! God had declared war on Satan and the deceiver intended to fight back.

One of Satan's most successful devices is *compromise.* If he can delude God's people into abandoning their privileged position of separation from sin and communion with God, then he can corrupt them and lead them into sin. He did this to Israel in the land of Moab (Num. 25; Ps. 106:28–31) and also after they had conquered the land of Canaan (Judg. 2; Ps. 106:34–48). The prophets warned the Jewish people not to compromise with the idolatrous worship of the pagans around them, but their warnings weren't heeded, and the nation experienced shameful defeat at the hands of their enemies.

What was Satan's plan for defeating God's people in Noah's day? To entice the godly line of Seth ("the sons of God") to mix with the ungodly line of Cain ("the daughters of men") and thus abandon their devotion to the Lord. It was the same temptation that Christians face today: be friendly with the world (James 4:4), love the world (1 John 2:15–17), and conform to the world (Rom. 12:2), rather than be separated from the world (2 Cor. 6:14–7:1). Of course, this could lead to being "condemned with the world" (1 Cor. 11:32). Lot is an example of this danger (Gen. 13; 19).

Some interpreters view 6:1–7 as an invasion of fallen angels who cohabited with women and produced a race of giants.[4] But as interesting as the theory is, it creates more problems than it solves, not the least of which is the union of sexless spirit beings with flesh and blood humans. Even if such unions did occur, could there be offspring and why would they be giants? And how did these "giants" (Nephilim, "fallen ones") survive the flood (v. 4; Num. 13:31–33), or was there a second invasion of fallen angels after the flood?

The term "sons of God" does refer to angels in Job 1:6; 2:1; 38:7, but these are *unfallen* angels faithfully serving God.[5] Even if fallen angels could make themselves appear in human bodies, why would they want to marry women and settle down on earth? Certainly their wives and neighbors would detect something different about them and this would create problems. Furthermore, the emphasis in Genesis 6 is on the sin of *man* and not the rebellion of angels. The word "man" is used nine times in verses 1–7, and God states clearly that the judgment was coming because of what humans had done. "And God saw that the wickedness of man was great in the earth" (v. 5).

The 120-year limit expressed in verse 3 probably refers to the years until the flood would come. God is long-suffering with lost sinners, but there comes a time when judgment must fall. During that "day of grace," Noah prepared the ark and gave witness that judgment was coming (2 Peter 2:5), the same message Enoch had given during his lifetime (Jude 14–15). God gave His message in the mouth of two witnesses, but the people wouldn't listen.

The word "giants" in Genesis 6:4 is a translation of the Hebrew word *nephilim* which means "fallen ones." Some who follow the "angel theory" of chapter 6 make the nephilim the fallen angels whose children became great leaders. As we've already seen, if these nephilim were angels with human bodies, then they either survived the flood (because the Hebrew spies saw them in Canaan; Num. 13:31–33), or there was a second invasion of "fallen angels" after the flood. Both ideas seem incredible.

The most likely interpretation of Genesis 6:4 is that God saw the people of that day as "fallen ones," while men saw these people as mighty leaders. Even today, much of what is admired by the world is rejected by the Lord (Luke 16:15). When the Sethites compromised by mingling with the Cainites, they fell from God's blessing. God was grieved that they married godless Cainites, choosing wives as they pleased without considering God's will (Gen. 6:2). In doing this, they endangered the fulfillment of the 3:15 promise, for how could God bring a Redeemer into the world through an unholy people? The people of that day were "marrying and giving in marriage" (Matt. 24:37–39) and thought nothing of the warning that Enoch and Noah gave about the coming judgment. Human history was now at the place where only Noah and his family—eight people—believed God and obeyed His Word. God's Spirit was striving with lost people, but they resisted the call of God, and God was grieved at what man was doing.[6]

Read Romans 1:17ff. for a description of what civilization was like in those days. Man's wickedness was great, every imagination of all his thoughts was *only* evil *continually,* so it was no surprise that God chose to send judgment.

Grace (v. 8). The only way people can be saved from God's wrath is through God's grace (Eph. 2:8–9), but grace isn't God's reward for a good life: It's God's response to saving faith. "By faith Noah, being divinely warned of things not yet seen, moved with godly fear, prepared an ark for the saving of his household" (Heb. 11:7 NKJV). True faith involves the whole of the inner person: The mind understands God's warning, the heart fears for what is coming, and the will acts in obedience to God's Word.

To understand God's truth but not act upon it is not biblical faith; it's only intellectual assent to religious truth. To be emotionally aroused without comprehending God's message isn't faith, because true faith is based on an understanding of the truth (Matt. 13:18–23). To have the mind enlightened and the heart stirred but not act in obedience to the message is not faith, for "faith without works is dead" (James 2:14–26). The mind, heart, and will are all involved in true biblical faith.

Everybody who has ever been saved from sin has been saved "by grace, through faith," and this includes the Old Testament worthies listed in Hebrews 11. Nobody was ever saved by bringing a sacrifice (Heb. 10:1–4; Ps. 51:16–17), by keeping the law (Gal. 2:16), or by doing good works (Rom. 4:5). Salvation is a gracious gift that can be rejected or received by faith. Like Noah, we must all find "grace in the eyes of the Lord" (Gen. 6:8).

QUESTIONS FOR PERSONAL REFLECTION
OR GROUP DISCUSSION

1. Which of the four special examples Wiersbe highlights—Seth, Enosh, Enoch, or Noah—encourages you the most? Why?

2. How is God's sovereign plan fulfilled when people so often choose to not obey God?

3. What light does the story of the very first human family shed on the family problems in our society?

4. Why does it again and again come down to a remnant left for the Lord? Why only a remnant?

5. When have you felt alone or failing in the work of the Lord?

6. How has the arrival of children affected your motivation, or that of someone you know, toward the Lord? How does knowledge of the second coming affect your motivation?

7. Wiersbe says one of Satan's most successful devices is compromise. In what areas of your life are you most vulnerable to compromise?

8. How can we tell the difference between those who are true mighty leaders and those who look mighty but are actually fallen?

9. Using the biblical data available, what do you imagine the world was like right before the flood?

10. In Old Testament times, what exactly did they need to believe to be saved?

Chapter Eight

ONE MAN'S FAITH, ONE MAN'S FAMILY

(Genesis 6:9—7:24)

Except for the increase in violence and crime, the times were pretty good. People were "eating and drinking, marrying and giving in marriage" (Matt. 24:38), and life was going on as usual. When friends met at the market or at wedding feasts, they laughed about Noah and his family ("Imagine building that big boat on dry land!") or discussed Methuselah, the world's oldest man ("He'll die one of these days, mark my word!"), or talked about Enoch, the man who suddenly disappeared ("Strangest thing I ever heard!").

Methuselah was Noah's grandfather, and Noah knew that when he died, nothing stood in the way of God's judgment falling on a wicked world. For over a century, Noah had been warning people about the coming judgment, but only his own family had believed him and trusted the Lord.

Then Methuselah died and things began to happen. One day, Noah and his family entered their "boat" and the rains came. ("It can't go on forever," people said. "It'll stop one of these days.") But it rained for forty days and forty nights, and subterranean explosions discharged more water on the earth. Even after the rain stopped, the water continued to rise, and within five months, the whole earth was under water and everything that breathed was dead. Everything, that is, except Noah and his family, the eight people everybody laughed at.

What kind of a person was Noah? He was the kind of person you and I should be and can be as we live in our world today.

A BELIEVING MAN WHO WALKED WITH GOD (6:9–13)

"But Noah found grace in the eyes of the Lord" (v. 8) introduces the third of the "generation" statements in Genesis: "These are the generations of Noah" (v. 9). Noah wasn't a minor character in the story of redemption; he's mentioned fifty times in eleven different books of the Bible.

Noah was a righteous man (v. 9; 7:1). This is the first time the word "righteous" is used in the Bible, but Noah's righteousness is also mentioned in other places (Ezek. 14:14, 20; Heb. 11:7; 2 Peter 2:5). Noah's righteousness didn't come from his good works; his good works came because of his righteousness. Like Abraham, his righteousness was God's gift in response to his personal faith. Both Abraham and Noah believed God's Word and it was "counted … to [them] for righteousness" (Gen. 15:6; see Heb. 11:7; Rom. 4:9ff.; Gal. 3:1ff.).

The only righteousness God will accept is the righteousness of Jesus Christ, His Son (2 Cor. 5:21), and the only way people can receive that righteousness is by admitting their sins and trusting Jesus Christ to save them (Rom. 3:19–30; Gal. 2:16). Noah must have learned this important truth from his father Lamech (Gen. 5:28–29), who learned it from his father Methuselah, who learned it from his father Enoch. How important it is to teach our children and grandchildren how to trust the Lord!

Noah was a blameless man (v. 9 NIV). If "righteous" describes Noah's standing before God, then "blameless" describes his conduct before people. "Blameless" doesn't mean "sinless," because nobody but Jesus Christ ever lived a sinless life on this earth (1 Peter 2:21–22). The word means "having integrity, whole, unblemished." It was used to describe the animals acceptable to God for sacrifice (Ex. 12:5; Lev. 1:3, 10). Noah's conduct was such that his neighbors couldn't find fault with him (Phil. 2:12–16).

The person who is right before God through faith in Christ ought to lead a life that is right before people, for faith without works is dead (James 2:14ff.). Paul warned about "unruly and vain talkers and deceivers … [who] profess that they know God; but in works they deny him" (Titus 1:10, 16). Noah wasn't that kind of person.

Noah was a man who walked with God (v. 9). His great-grandfather Enoch had "walked with God" and was suddenly taken to heaven and rescued from the impending judgment of the flood (5:24). Noah walked with God and was taken safely through the judgment. Enoch modeled a godly way of life for Methuselah. Methuselah must have passed it along to his son Lamech who shared it with his son Noah. How wonderful it is when generation after generation in one family is faithful to the Lord, especially at a time in history when violence and corruption are the normal way of life.

The life of faith and obedience is compared to a "walk" because this life begins with one step: trusting Jesus Christ as Lord and Savior. This step of faith leads to a daily walk, a step at a time, as the Lord directs us. He commands us to "walk in love" (Eph. 5:2), "walk as children of light" (v. 8), "walk in the Spirit" (Gal. 5:16, 25), and "walk circumspectly [carefully]" (Eph. 5:15). A step at a time, a day at a time, we walk with the Lord, and He guides us into His will and blesses us with His wisdom and strength.

Noah was an obedient man (v. 22; 7:5, 16). One of the major messages in Scripture is that we must not only hear God's Word but we must also obey it (James 1:22–25). Because Noah was obedient to the Lord, his "house" wasn't destroyed when the storm came (Matt. 7:24–27). It wasn't easy for Noah and his family to obey the Lord, because the rest of the population was disobeying God and rebelling against His will. According to Enoch, they were ungodly people committing ungodly deeds in ungodly ways and speaking ungodly words against the Lord God (Jude 15).

Whether it has to do with sexual abstinence, using alcohol and drugs, or joining gangs and breaking the law, we hear a great deal today about "peer pressure." It's the excuse for all kinds of illegal and immoral behavior, from cheating on your income tax to cheating on your spouse. But anybody who has ever developed godly character has had to fight against peer pressure, including Noah and his family, Abraham and his family, Moses in Egypt (Heb. 11:24–26), and Daniel and his friends in Babylon (Dan. 1). Resisting peer pressure means not only saying a determined no to people but also a dedicated yes to the Lord (Rom. 12:1–2).

Most people know that Noah built an ark. What they may not know is that he also built a godly character and a godly family. Had it not been for Noah's godly family, Abraham wouldn't have been born, and without Abraham, would there have been a Jewish nation, the Bible, and the Savior?

A Faithful Man who Worked for God (6:14–22)

"The secret of the Lord is with them that fear him; and he will [show] them his covenant" (Ps. 25:14). When you walk with God, He speaks to you through His Word and tells you what you need to know and to do. Christians are more than just servants who do His will; we're also His friends who know His plans (John 15:14–15). God's plan involved three responsibilities for Noah and his family.

Building an ark (vv. 14–17). God told Noah what his task was: to build a wooden vessel that would survive the waters of the flood and keep Noah and his family safe. If the cubit mentioned was the standard cubit of eighteen inches, then the vessel was 450 feet long, seventy-five feet wide, and forty-five feet high. It had three decks, one door, and a series of small windows eighteen inches high right under the roof, providing light and ventilation. The three decks were divided into compartments (Gen. 6:14) where the various animals would be kept and where Noah and his family would live.

This vessel was designed for flotation, not navigation. It was a huge wooden box that could float on the water and keep the contents safe and dry. Dr. Henry Morris calculated that the ark was large enough to hold the contents of over 500 livestock railroad cars, providing space for about 125,000 animals. Of course, many of the animals would be very small and not need much space, and when it came to the large animals, Noah no doubt collected younger and smaller representatives.[1] There was plenty of room in the vessel for food for both humans and animals (v. 21), and the insects and creeping things would have no problem finding places to live on the ark.

Trusting God's covenant (v. 18). This is the first use of the word "covenant" in the Bible. The word appears often in Scripture because the covenant concept is an important part of God's great plan of redemption. (God would explain His covenant to Noah after he left the ark; 8:20–9:17.) A covenant is an agreement that involves obligations and benefits for the parties involved. In some of the covenants, God alone is the "covenant party" and makes unconditional promises to His people. But there were also covenants that required His people to fulfill certain conditions before God could bless them.

God's words in 6:13–21 were addressed specifically to Noah, but God also included Noah's family in the covenant (v. 18). Noah didn't become a father until he was 500 years old (5:32), and he entered the ark when he was 600 (7:6); so his three sons were still "young" as far as pre-flood ages were concerned. Ham was the youngest son (9:22–24) and Japheth was the eldest (10:21), and all three boys were married (7:13).[2]

The fact that God had covenanted to care for Noah and his family gave them the peace and confidence they needed as they prepared the ark and then lived in it for over a year. God is faithful to keep His promises, and as God's covenant people, the eight believers had nothing to fear.

Gathering the animals (vv. 19–22). God not only wanted humans to be preserved from destruction but also every kind of creature that would be drowned by the waters of the flood. But how was Noah to gather such a large number of animals, birds, and creeping things? God would cause these creatures to come to Noah (v. 20; 7:8–9, 15), and Noah would take them into the ark (6:19). This included not only pairs of unclean animals who would be able to reproduce after the flood, but also seven pairs of clean animals (7:2), some of whom would be used for sacrifices (8:20). Noah and his family not only learned about the faithfulness of God, but they also saw the sovereignty of God in action.

In His sovereign power, God brought the animals to Noah and his sons and controlled them so that they did His bidding. However, this magnificent demonstration of God's power didn't touch the hearts of his neighbors, and they perished in the flood. The birds, beasts, and creeping things knew their Creator's voice and obeyed Him, but people made in the image of God refused to heed God's call. Centuries later, God would say through His servant Isaiah, "The ox knows his master, the donkey his owner's manger, but Israel does not know, my people do not understand" (Isa. 1:3 NIV).

During all of this important activity, Noah was serving the Lord and bearing witness to a sinful world. For 120 years (Gen. 6:3), God was long-suffering toward careless and rebellious sinners, but they ignored His message and lost their opportunity for salvation.

A SECURE MAN WHO WAITED ON GOD (7:1–24)

"Do not be like the horse or the mule," God counsels in Psalm 32:9 (NIV), and Noah obeyed that counsel. The horse sometimes wants to rush ahead impetuously, and the mule wants to drag its feet and stubbornly stay back;

but Noah walked with God and worked for God and let God arrange the schedule.

A week of waiting (vv. 1–10). Since the rains started on the seventeenth day of the second month (Gen. 7:11), it was on the tenth day of the second month that Noah and his family moved into the ark at God's instruction (v. 1). During that final week before the flood, they finished gathering the animals and putting in their supplies. They followed the Lord's instructions, trusted His covenant promise, and knew that there was nothing to fear.

David watched a thunderstorm one day and from that experience wrote a hymn (Ps. 29) telling how he had seen and heard God in that storm. As he pondered what happened, David thought about history's most famous storm in the time of Noah, and he wrote, "The Lord sat enthroned at the Flood, and the Lord sits as King forever" (v. 10 NKJV). The sweeping rain, the echoing thunder, and the flashing lightning reminded David of the sovereignty of God. No matter how great the storms of life may be, God is still on the throne causing everything to work together for good. That's why David ended his hymn with, "The Lord will give strength to His people; the Lord will bless His people with peace" (v. 11 NKJV).

At the end of that final week of preparation, Noah and his family obeyed God's command and entered the ark, and God shut the door and made it safe (Gen. 7:16). They didn't know how long they would live in the ark, but the Lord knew, and that's really all that mattered. "My times are in Your hand" (Ps. 31:15 NKJV). One year and ten days later, the same God opened the door and invited them to come out to live on His freshly cleansed earth (Gen. 8:16).

The day of reckoning (7:11–24). The flood was God's judgment of a wicked world. God opened the floodgates of heaven so that torrential rains came down, and "all the springs of the great deep burst forth" (v. 11 NIV), so that even the highest mountains were covered by water (v. 20). God had waited for over a century for sinners to repent, and now it was too late. "Seek the Lord while he may be found, call upon him while he is near" (Isa. 55:6).

The rain stopped after forty days, which would be on the twenty-eighth day of the third month (Gen. 7:12). However, the water continued to rise for another 110 days and reached its peak after 150 days (v. 24). At that time, the ark rested on a mountain peak of Ararat (8:4). It would take 150 days for the water to recede (v. 3), which takes us to the twelfth month, the seventeenth day. Two months and ten days later, Noah and his family left the ark and set the animals free (8:15–19). From the day that God shut them in, they had been in the ark a year and ten days.

A universal judgment. In recent years, people who want to accommodate Scripture to the views of modern science have opted for a flood that was "limited" and not universal. They suggest that the writer of Genesis used "the language of appearance" and described only what he could see.

There are problems with both views, but the "limited" interpretation seems to be the weaker of the two.[3] The clear language of the text seems to state that God was bringing a universal judgment. God said He would destroy humans and beasts "from the face of the earth" (6:7),[4] and that "every living thing" would be destroyed (7:4, 21–23; 8:21 NASB). If the mountains were covered to such a height that the ark could float over the Ararat range and eventually settle down on a peak, then the entire planet must have been completely immersed (7:18–20). A person reading Genesis 6—9 for the first time would conclude that the flood was universal.

But if the flood was not universal, why did God give the rainbow as a universal sign of His covenant? (9:11–15) Why would people in a local area need such a sign? Furthermore, if the flood was a local event, why did God tell Noah to build such a big vessel for saving his family and the animals? Noah certainly had enough time to gather together his family and the animals in that area and lead them to a place where the flood wouldn't reach them.[5]

God promised that He would never send another flood like the one He sent in Noah's day (vv. 8–17). But if the flood was only a local event, God didn't keep His promise! Over the centuries, there have been numerous local floods, some of which brought death and devastation to localities. In 1996 alone, massive flooding in Afghanistan in April left 3,000 people homeless; and in July, flooding in Northern Bangladesh destroyed the homes of over 2 million people. In July and August, the Yellow, Yangtze, and Hai rivers flooded nine provinces in China and left 2,000 people dead. If Noah's flood was a local event like these floods, then God's promise and the covenant sign of the rainbow mean nothing.

The plain reading of the text convinces us that the flood was a universal judgment because "all flesh had corrupted his [God's] way upon the earth" (6:12). We don't know how far civilization had spread over the planet, but wherever humans went, there was sin that had to be judged. The flood bears witness to universal sin and universal judgment.

Both Jesus and Peter used the flood to illustrate future events that will involve the whole world: the return of Christ (Matt. 24:37–39; Luke 17:26–27) and the worldwide judgment of fire (2 Peter 3:3–7). If the flood was only local, these analogies are false and misleading. Peter also wrote that God did not spare "the ancient world" (2 Peter 2:5 NKJV) when He sent the flood, which implies much more territory than a limited area.

A patient family. In spite of the devastation on the outside, Noah and his family and the animals were secure inside the ark. No matter how they felt, or how much the ark was tossed on the waters, they were safe in God's will. Patiently they waited for God to complete His work and put them back on the earth. Noah and his family spent one year and seventeen days in the ark, and even though they had daily chores to do, that's a long time to be in one place. But it is "through faith and patience" that we inherit God's promised blessings (Heb. 6:12; see 10:36), and Noah was willing to wait on the Lord.

Peter saw in Noah's experience a picture of salvation through faith in Jesus Christ (1 Peter 3:18–22). The earth in Noah's day was immersed in water, but the ark floated above the water and brought Noah and his family to the place of safety. This was, to Peter, a picture of baptism: death, burial, and resurrection. The earth was "dead" and "buried" because of the water, but the ark rose up ("resurrection") to bring the family through safely.[6] Jesus died, was buried, and arose again, and through His finished work, we have salvation from sin. Peter makes it clear that the water of baptism doesn't wash away sin. It's our obedience to the Lord's command to be baptized (Matt. 28:19–20) that cleanses the conscience so that we are right before God.

The British expositor Alexander Maclaren said:

For a hundred and twenty years the wits laughed, and the "common-sense" people wondered, and the patient saint went on hammering and pitching at his ark. But one morning it began to rain; and by degrees, somehow, Noah did not seem quite such a fool. The jests would look rather different when the water was up to the knees of the jesters; and their sarcasms would stick in their throats as they drowned.

So is it always. So it will be at the last great day. The men who lived for the future, by faith in Christ, will be found out to have been the wise men when the future has become the present, and the present has become the past, and is gone for ever; while they who had no aims beyond the things of time, which are now sunk beneath the dreary horizon, will awake too late to the conviction that they are outside the ark of safety, and that their truest epitaph is, "Thou fool."[7]

QUESTIONS FOR PERSONAL REFLECTION
OR GROUP DISCUSSION

1. How can a person receive or develop a strong faith like that of Noah?

2. When a professed believer is not leading "a life that is right before people," what do we say to that person? How should we interact with them?

3. How can local churches help families pass on the faith from generation to generation?

4. What does it mean to "walk" with God? In what ways is "walking" a helpful picture of the life we're meant to live?

5. What types of peer pressure do you have to resist? What helps you to be successful in your effort?

6. Noah was faced with what looked like an impossible task: building an ark. But he began it in faith. What task are you facing that you need faith to get started or to continue?

7. Which of God's promises give you peace and confidence?

8. What is the difference between humans and animals when it comes to hearing and obeying the Lord?

9. What does God's decision to send the flood tell you about Him?

10. How would you defend the reality of the flood to a skeptic?

Chapter Nine

The God of New Beginnings

(Genesis 8)

W hen anxious believers are searching the Bible for something encouraging to read, they're more likely to turn to Romans 8 than to Genesis 8. After all, Romans 8 is one of the most heartening chapters in Scripture, while Genesis 8 describes God's "mop-up" operation after the flood.

But the next time you find yourself in a storm, Genesis 8 can give you new hope and encouragement, because the major theme of the chapter is renewal and rest after tribulation. The chapter records the end of a storm and the beginning of new life and hope for God's people and God's creation. Just consider what God does in Genesis 8 and take courage!

God Remembers His Own (8:1a)

When you're going through a storm, it's easy to feel forsaken. "I think the Lord has forgotten me," said a church member whom I was visiting in the hospital. In her mind, she could recall Hebrews 13:5 and quote it ("I will never leave you nor forsake you" [NKJV]); but in her heart, she felt lonely and abandoned. Where was her God? When would the storm end?

Feeling forsaken is a normal human emotion that most of us have experienced, whether we admit it or not. "Why do You stand afar off, O Lord?" asked the psalmist. "Why do You hide in times of trouble?" (Ps. 10:1 NKJV). Paul confessed that his troubles in Asia had been so severe that he almost gave up on life (2 Cor. 1:8), and Jesus, who experienced all our human trials, cried from the cross, "My God, My God, why have You forsaken Me?" (Matt. 27:46 NKJV). Feeling desolate is nothing new to the people of God; but then they recall the song:

> God is still on the throne,
> And He will remember His own!

The word "remember" in Genesis 8:1 doesn't mean to call something to mind that may have been forgotten. God can't forget anything because He knows the end from the beginning. Rather, it means "to pay attention to, to fulfill a promise and act on behalf of somebody." For example, God's promise "and their sins and iniquities will I remember no more" (Heb. 10:17) means that God doesn't hold our sins against us and treat us as sinners. Certainly God knows what we've done, but because of our faith in Jesus Christ, our sins are "forgotten." God deals with us as though our sins had never been committed! The Lord remembers them against us no more.

To remember means to act on behalf of another. God remembered Abraham and rescued Lot from destruction in Sodom (Gen. 19:29). The Lord remembered both Rachel and Hannah and enabled them to conceive and bear sons (30:22; 1 Sam. 1:11, 19). The Lord remembered His covenant and delivered the Jews from the bondage of Egypt (Ex. 2:24; 6:5). "To remember" implies a previous commitment made by God and announces the fulfillment of that commitment.[1] Noah, his family, and the animals had been together in the ark for over a year, which is a lot of "togetherness." Did they ever get impatient with each other or with the animals? There's no record that God spoke to them after He had shut them into the ark, so perhaps somebody in the family experienced an occasional fleeting fear that maybe God didn't care for them anymore.

God not only remembered Noah and his family, but He also remembered the animals that were with them in the ark.[2] God spared these creatures so they could live on the renewed earth and reproduce after their kind. It was His desire that His creatures enjoy the earth and contribute to the happiness of the people He had created in His own image. As we shall see later, the animals were included in God's covenant with Noah.

We can be sure that God never forgets or forsakes His people, not only because of His promises,[3] but also because of His character. God is love, and where there's love, there's faithfulness. He can never deny Himself or His Word, for He's the faithful God, and He can never change, because He's immutable. Because He's perfect, God can't change for the better; and because He's holy, He can't change for the worse. We can depend on Him no matter what our circumstances or no matter how we feel.

GOD RENEWS HIS WORLD (8:1B–14)

According to 7:24, the flood reached its peak in 150 days. The torrential rain and the eruptions of water from beneath the earth had both ceased (8:2; see NIV and NASB), and during the next five months, God caused the water to recede and leave the dry land behind.

Where did the floodwaters go? Never underestimate the power of moving water! It's possible that the flood greatly altered the contours of the land and created new areas for the water to fill, both on the surface of the earth and underground.[4] Since there were eruptions from beneath the earth (7:11), whole continents and mountain ranges could have risen and fallen, creating huge areas into which the water could spill. The winds that God sent over the earth helped to evaporate the water and also move it to the places God had provided. A God powerful enough to cover the earth with water is also wise enough to know how to dispose of it when its work is done.

Centuries later, God's wind would bring the locusts into Egypt and later drive them into the sea (Ex. 10:10–20). God's wind would also open up the Red Sea and make a dry path for the people of Israel as they left Egypt (14:21–22; 15:10). The stormy wind fulfills God's word (Ps. 148:8).

On the seventeenth day of the seventh month, the ark rested on a peak in the mountains of Ararat, located in modern Turkey. We don't know which peak it was; explorers searching for the remains of the ark can't find much biblical data to help them. In later years, the seventh month was very special to the Jews, for during that month they ushered in the new year with the Feast of Trumpets and celebrated the Day of Atonement and the Feast of Tabernacles (Lev. 23:23–44).[5]

The Hebrew text says that "the ark came to rest," reminding us that Noah's name means "rest" and that his father Lamech had hoped that his son would bring rest to a weary world (Gen. 5:28–29). Though the ark had rested safely, Noah was waiting for the Lord to tell him what to do. He waited forty days and then sent out the raven; and being an unclean carrion-eating bird (Lev. 11:13–15), it felt right at home among the floating carcasses.

Noah waited a week and then sent out a dove, which, being a clean bird, found no place to land; so it returned to the ark (Gen. 8:8–9). A week later Noah sent the dove out again, and when it returned with a fresh olive leaf, Noah knew that the plants were growing and fresh life had appeared on the earth (vv. 10–11). A dove bearing an olive branch is a familiar symbol of peace around the world. A week later, when Noah sent the dove out the third time, it didn't return; so he knew the water had dried up.[6]

Noah had built a "window" (hatch?) in the upper deck of the ark (v. 13 NIV reads "covering"), and this he opened so he could survey the world around him. This was on the day the passengers had been in the ark one entire year. Noah saw that the ground indeed was dry, but he didn't make a move out of the ark until the Lord told him to leave. Twenty-six days later, that order came and he obeyed it (vv. 15–19).

GOD REWARDS FAITH (8:15–19)

Noah was a man of faith whose name is recorded in Hebrews 11 with those of other heroes of faith (v. 7). He had the faith to walk with God when the people of the world were ignoring and disobeying God. He had the faith to work for God and to witness for God when opposition to truth was the popular thing. Now that the flood was over, he exercised faith to wait on God before leaving the ark.

After being confined to the ark for over a year, he and his family must have yearned to get back on dry land, but they waited for God's directions. Circumstances on the earth looked suitable for their disembarking, but that was no guarantee that God wanted them to exit immediately and begin their new life. Obedient faith is our response to God's Word, for "faith comes by hearing, and hearing by the word of God" (Rom. 10:17 NKJV).

Was Noah revealing unbelief when he sent out the birds or opened the hatch to look at the terrain? No, he was simply using available opportunities to gather data. It isn't wrong to have an understanding of the situation; just don't lean on your own understanding (Prov. 3:5–6). Obeying the will of God involves not only doing the right thing in the right way for the right motive, but it also means doing it a*t the right time.* "My times are in Your hand" (Ps. 31:15 NKJV).

God rewarded Noah's faith, and the faith of his family, by caring for them in the ark for over a year and then preparing the earth for them so that they could leave the ark. Noah was like a "second Adam" as he made this new beginning for the human race. God had brought the earth out of the waters during creation week, preparing it for Adam and Eve, and now He had brought the earth through the flood and made it ready for

Noah and his family. The Lord even gave Noah's family and the animals the same mandate that He had given at the beginning: "Be fruitful, and multiply" (Gen. 8:17; 1:22, 28).

Noah prepared the ark "for the saving of his household" (Heb. 11:7 NKJV), and God was faithful to save his household. There's no indication in Scripture that Noah in his witnessing invited others to join him and his family in the ark, but he certainly must have encouraged them to trust God and prepare their own arks. Of course, nobody took his message seriously, and the world of that day perished (2 Peter 3:6).

What was it that caused the population to reject God's word and perish? They were like the people in our Lord's parable (Luke 14:16–24) who were occupied with the ordinary things of daily life (Matt. 24:37–39) and unconcerned about eternity. They believed that life would go on as it always had and that nothing would change. They said that God wouldn't invade the world or interrupt the scheme of things, but He did! People today have the same attitude concerning the return of the Lord (2 Peter 3:1–9; 1 Thess. 5:1–10).

When it comes to saving faith, each of us must trust Jesus Christ personally; we can't be saved by the faith of a substitute. Noah's wife, their three sons, and their three daughters-in-law were also believers; and they proved it by standing with Noah while he worked and witnessed, and then by entering the ark in obedience to the Lord.[7]

God Receives Worship (8:20)

After he stepped out of the ark and stood on the renewed earth, Noah was so filled with gratitude that his first act was to lead his family in worship. He built an altar and offered some of the clean animals as sacrifices to the Lord.

Noah was a balanced believer. He walked with the Lord in loving communion and enjoyed His presence. He worked for the Lord in building the ark, and he witnessed for the Lord as "a preacher of righteousness"

(2 Peter 2:5). While in the ark, he waited on the Lord for instructions concerning his leaving, and once he was standing on the earth, he worshipped the Lord. Like Abel, he brought God his very best (Gen. 4:4), and like the Sethite remnant, he called on the name of the Lord (v. 26). The true worship of the Lord had been restored on the earth.

In Old Testament days, when you sacrificed a burnt offering, you gave the entire animal or bird to the Lord with nothing kept back (Lev. 1). "All on the altar" (v. 9) was the biblical law, because the sacrifice symbolized total dedication to the Lord.[8] In a new step of commitment, Noah gave himself and his family completely to the Lord. God had graciously protected them and brought them through the storm, so it was only fitting that they make themselves available to the Lord to do His will.

The description of God "smell[ing] the pleasing aroma" (Gen. 8:21 NIV) is a human way of stating a divine truth: God was satisfied with the sacrifice, accepted it, and was pleased with His people and their worship (Lev. 1:9; 3:16). If God refused to "smell" the fragrance of the offering, it meant that He was displeased with the worshippers (Lev. 26:31; Isa. 1:11–15).[9] In New Testament language, the sacrifice speaks of Jesus Christ offering Himself up for us. "And walk in love, as Christ also has loved us and given Himself for us, an offering and a sacrifice to God for a sweet-smelling aroma" (Eph. 5:2 NKJV).

In and of ourselves, we can't please God by what we are or by what we do, but by faith, we can be accepted in Jesus Christ. The Father said of Jesus, "This is my beloved Son, in whom I am well pleased" (Matt. 3:17). Those who put their faith in Christ are "in Christ" (2 Cor. 5:17), and when the Father looks at them, He sees the righteousness of His Son (v. 21). Believers are "accepted in the beloved" Son who is well-pleasing to the Father (Eph. 1:6).

Like the ark that saved Noah and his family, Jesus Christ went through the storm of God's judgment for us. Jonah, who is a type of Christ in death, burial, and resurrection (Matt. 12:38–40), went through the storm of God's wrath because of his disobedience, but Jesus went through the storm in obedience to God's will. Jesus could say, "All thy waves and thy billows are gone over me" (Ps. 42:7; Jonah 2:3). Our Lord's suffering on the cross was the "baptism" Jesus referred to in Luke 12:50 and that was pictured when John baptized Jesus in the Jordan River.

GOD REAFFIRMS THE NATURAL ORDER (8:21–22)

The Lord didn't speak these words to Noah; He spoke them to Himself in His own heart. It was His gracious response to Noah's faith, obedience, and worship. What did God promise?

The ground cursed no more (v. 21a). God had cursed the ground because of Adam's sin (3:17) and had added a further curse because of Cain's sins (4:11–12). God's promise recorded here didn't invalidate either of those curses, and they won't be removed until Jesus returns and God's people dwell in the Holy City (Rev. 22:3). But in His grace, God decided not to add to man's affliction.

No more universal floods (v. 21b). God also determined that there would be no future floods. God's reason given in verse 21 has been variously explained, and the explanation depends to some degree on your translation of the text. Did God say "for the imagination of man's heart is evil" (KJV, NKJV), or did He say "even though every inclination of his heart is evil" (NIV)? The Lord had originally sent the flood because of the evil hearts of the people (6:5), so not to send another judgment would make it look like the flood was a mistake or a failure, or that God had given up on the human race created in His own image.

If we translate 8:21 "for," then we have God saying, "The human heart is incurably wicked. The flood wiped out the transgressors, but it couldn't change hearts. Therefore, to have another judgment won't solve the problem." If we translate it "even though," then we have God saying: "Yes, they deserve judgment because their hearts are wicked. And to persist in sin and not learn their lesson from this flood only shows how evil they are. But in grace, I will not send another flood or curse the ground."

Perhaps both are true. The important thing is that God spoke these words in response to Noah's sacrifice, and that the sacrifice was a picture of the sacrifice of Christ (Heb. 10:1–10; Eph. 5:2). On the basis of the atonement accomplished by Jesus Christ on the cross, God could say, "A price has been paid for the sins of the world, and I can withhold judgment. Justice has been met, My law has been upheld, and I can show grace to a lost world. I will not send another flood and wipe out the human race. Instead, I will offer them My great salvation."

This doesn't mean that God doesn't judge sin today or that there will be no future judgment of the world. Romans 1:18ff. makes it clear that God's judgment is being revealed against sinners right now through the consequences of their sins. God gave them over to their own sinful bondage and gave them up to the consequences of their sins in their own bodies. One of the greatest judgments God can send to sinners is to let them have their own way *and then pay for it in their own lives.* That's the judgment the world is experiencing right now. There will be a future global judgment, but not a judgment of water; it will be a judgment of fire (2 Peter 3).

No interruption of the cycle of nature (v. 22). The flood had interrupted the normal cycle of the seasons for a year, but that would never be repeated. Instead, God reaffirmed that the rhythm of days and weeks and seasons would continue as long as the earth endured. Without this guarantee, mankind could never be sure of having the necessities of life.

We know now that the steady cycle of days and nights, weeks and months, seasons and years, is maintained by the rotation of the earth on its axis and the orbit of the earth around the sun. God made it that way so that His universe would operate effectively. Although there were myriads of galaxies to choose from, the Lord chose to pour His love and grace down upon the inhabitants of the earth. "The earth is the Lord's" (Ps. 24:1). The Lord so arranged the universe that the living things on earth might be maintained, and this includes men and women who too often forget God's care.

The guarantee in Genesis 8:22 gives us hope and courage as we face an unknown future. Each time we go to bed for the night, or turn the calendar to a new month, we should be reminded that God is concerned about planet earth and its inhabitants. With the invention of the electric light and modern means of transportation and communication, our world has moved away from living by the cycles of nature established by God. We no longer go to bed at sundown and get up at sunrise, and if we don't like the weather where we are, we can quickly travel to a different climate. But if God were to dim the sun, rearrange the seasons, or tilt the earth at a different angle, our lives would be in jeopardy.

God invites us to live a day at a time. Jesus taught us to pray, "Give us this day our daily bread" (Matt. 6:11) and to be thankful for it. "As your days, so shall your strength be" (Deut. 33:25 NKJV; see Matt. 6:25–34). When His disciples warned Jesus not to go to Bethany, He replied, "Are there not twelve hours in the day?" (John 11:9). He obeyed the Father's schedule and lived a day at a time, trusting the Father to care for Him.

God's "covenant of day and night" is especially meaningful to the people of Israel, for it guarantees them His care and protection so that they will never cease to be a nation (Jer. 33:19–26). God's promise that He will not send another flood is assurance to the Jews that His covenant with them will never be broken (Isa. 54:7–10).

We're prone to take for granted sunrise and sunset, the changing face of the moon and the changing seasons, but all of these functions are but evidences that God is on the throne and keeping His promises. All creation preaches a constant sermon, day after day, season after season, that assures us of God's loving care. We can trust His Word, for "there has not failed one word of all His good promise" (1 Kings 8:56 NKJV).

QUESTIONS FOR PERSONAL REFLECTION OR GROUP DISCUSSION

1. Why would it be of special benefit to read Genesis 8 when you're in one of life's storms?

2. When is it easy to feel forsaken by God? How can you help someone who is feeling this way?

3. What can we learn from God's example of "not remembering" our sins as we seek to forgive others?

4. How can the truth of God's immutability help us as we travel the ups and downs of life?

5. Noah had to wait on God until the flood was over. When have you had to wait on God's timing? Why was that necessary?

6. At what times do you find yourself, like people in Noah's day, too occupied with the ordinary things of daily life?

7. How can we encourage one another to resist this trap of being caught up with the ordinary?

8. Genesis 8:21 says God was smelling the pleasant aroma. What other anthropomorphisms can you recall from the Bible?

9. Why did God make the promise not to send another worldwide flood?

10. What comfort can you derive from God's promise to continue the normal cycles of seasons?

Chapter Ten

To Life! To Life!

(Genesis 9:1–17)

To Life" is one of the happiest songs in *Fiddler on the Roof,* the musical that dramatizes Jewish life in the little village of Anatevka. The milkman, Tevye, and his neighbors were defenseless, poor, and unsure of their future in czarist Russia, yet they still celebrated life as a joyful gift from a generous God. Whether it was the announcement of an engagement, the birth of a baby, or even the arrival of a sewing machine, the humble residents of Anatevka found reasons to give thanks for the blessings of life.

In this passage (Gen. 9:1–17), God addressed the eight survivors of the flood and gave them instructions concerning four areas of life. Though given initially to Noah and his family, these instructions apply to all people in all ages and all places. They are permanent ordinances from God for all humanity, and they must not be ignored or altered. Life is precious, and it must be handled with care.

Multiplying Life (9:1, 7)

When Noah came out of the ark, he was like a "second Adam" about to usher in a new beginning on earth for the human race. Faith in the Lord had saved Noah and his household from destruction, and his three sons would repopulate the whole earth (v. 18).

God had told Adam and Eve to "be fruitful, and multiply, and replenish the earth" (1:28), and He repeated that mandate *twice* to Noah and his family (9:1, 7). All of Noah's descendants were important to the plan of God, but especially the line of Shem. From that line Abraham would be born, the man God chose to found the Jewish nation. From that nation would come the Redeemer who would fulfill 3:15 and crush the serpent's head.

In Scripture, children are described as a blessing, not a curse, and to have many children and grandchildren was evidence of the favor of God (Gen. 24:60; Ps. 127:3–5; 128:3–4). God promised Abraham that his descendants would be as the stars of the sky and the sand of the sea (Gen. 15:5; 22:17), and the patriarchs invoked the blessing of fruitfulness on their heirs (28:3; 35:11; 48:4). The Lord covenanted with Israel to give them many children if the nation would obey His laws (Lev. 26:9; Deut. 7:13).

Many people today don't seem to have that attitude toward children. In nearly 200 years of American history, starting with the Revolutionary War, 1.2 million military personnel have been killed in nine major wars. But in *one year* in the United States, 1.6 million babies are legally aborted.[1] In biblical times, Jewish couples wouldn't have considered aborting a child, no matter how difficult their circumstances or meager their resources. Life was God's gift and children were a heritage from the Lord, treasures to be protected and invested for His glory.

SUSTAINING LIFE (9:2–4)

A survey taken in 1900 revealed that people felt they needed seventy-two things in order to function normally and be content. Fifty years later, in a similar survey, the total came to nearly 500 things! But the Bible lists only two: "And having food and clothing, with these we shall be content" (1 Tim. 6:8 NKJV).

In the Sermon on the Mount, Jesus taught the same truth when He spoke about the birds and the flowers (Matt. 6:24–34). If the heavenly Father clothes the flowers with beauty and gives the birds their food, surely He will provide food and raiment for His own dearly loved children. "For your heavenly Father knows that you need all these things" (v. 32 NKJV).

When God established Adam and Eve in their garden home, He gave them fruit and plants to eat (Gen. 1:29; 2:9, 16); but after the flood, He expanded the human diet to include meat. The harmony in nature that Adam and Eve had enjoyed was now gone, for Noah and his family didn't have "dominion" over animal life (1:26, 28). Now the animals would fear humans and do everything possible to escape the threat of death. Since most animals reproduce rapidly and their young mature quickly, the beasts could easily overrun the human population; so God put the fear of humans into the animals. Cain was a farmer, Abel was a shepherd, but Noah and his sons were now hunters.

However, God put one restriction on the eating of animal flesh: The meat must be free of blood (9:4). God stated concisely to Noah what He later elaborated through Moses: The life is in the blood, and the life must be respected, even if you're butchering an animal to eat at a feast. (See Lev. 3:17; 7:26–27; 17:10–14; 19:26; Deut. 12:16, 23–25; 15:23.)[2] In this restriction, God revealed again His concern for animal life. The life is in the blood, and that life comes from God and should be respected. Furthermore, the blood of animals would be important in most of the Mosaic sacrifices, so the blood must be treated with reverence.

Jesus taught that it was permissible to eat all foods (Mark 7:1–23), and both Peter (Acts 10) and Paul (1 Tim. 4:3–4; Col. 2:16) reaffirmed this truth. However, the early church still faced disagreements over diets (Rom. 14:1—15:7). To keep Gentile believers from offending Jewish believers or seekers, the early Christians were advised not to be careless about the eating of meat (Acts 15:19–21, 24–29).[3] Paul's counsel was: receive one another, love one another, do nothing to make one another stumble, and seek to build one another up in the faith. The approach was love; the goal was maturity.

PROTECTING LIFE (9:5–6)

From instructing Noah about the shedding of animal blood, the Lord proceeded to discuss an even more important topic: the shedding of human blood. Thus far, mankind didn't have a very good track record when it came to caring for one another. Cain had killed his brother Abel (4:8), Lamech had killed a young man and bragged about it (vv. 23–24), and the earth had been filled with all kinds of violence (6:11, 13). God had put the fear of humans into the animals, but now He had to put the fear of God into the humans lest they destroy one another!

Those who kill their fellow human beings will have to answer to God for their deeds, for men and women are made in the image of God.[4] To attack a human being is to attack God, and the Lord will bring judgment on the offender. All life is the gift of God, and to take away life means to take the place of God. The Lord gives life and He alone has the right to authorize taking it away (Job 1:21).

But how did God arrange to punish murderers and see that justice is done and the law upheld? He established human government on the earth and in so doing shared with mankind the awesome power of taking human life. That's the import of God's mandate in Genesis 9:6. Human government and capital punishment go together, as Paul explains in Romans 13:1–7. Government authorities carry the sword and have the right to use it.

Under Old Testament law there was no police force as we know it. If a murder was committed, it was up to the family of the victim to find the culprit and bring him to justice. There's a difference between murder and involuntary manslaughter (Ex. 21:12–14), so the Lord instructed the nation of Israel to establish six cities of refuge to which an accused murderer could flee for safety (Num. 35:6–34; Deut. 19:1–13). The elders of the city would protect the accused until the case could be investigated, and if the accused was found guilty, the family of the deceased could proceed with the execution. Since the murderer had shed blood, the murderer's blood must be shed.

Government was established by God because the human heart is evil (Gen. 6:5) and the fear of punishment can help to restrain would-be law-breakers. The law can restrain but it can't regenerate; only the grace of God can change the human heart (Jer. 31:31–34; Heb. 8:7–13). But if individuals, families, or groups were allowed to deal with offenders in their own way, society would be in a state of constant chaos. Human government has its weaknesses and limitations, but government is better than anarchy and people doing what's right in their own eyes (Judg. 17:6; 18:1; 19:1; 21:25).[5]

God ordained and established three institutions on this earth: marriage and the family (Gen. 1:26–28; 2:18–25), human government (9:5–6), and the church (Matt. 16:13–19; Acts 2). Each has its sphere of responsibility and one can't substitute for the other. The church wields the sword of the Spirit (Heb. 4:12), not the sword of justice (Rom. 13:4; John 18:36), but if the government interferes with matters of Christian conscience, believers have the right to disobey (Acts 4:18–20).

Opponents of capital punishment ask, "Does capital punishment deter crime?" But does *any law* deter crime, including parking laws and speed laws? Perhaps not as much as we'd desire, but the punishment of offenders does help society to honor law and justice. Nobody knows how many people learn about convictions and think twice before they disobey the law. The law also helps to protect and compensate innocent people who are victims of lawless behavior.

Not everything that's legal is biblical. Regardless of what philosophers, parliaments, and courts may say, God's mandate of capital punishment begins with "whoever." It was given by God to be respected and obeyed by all people.

Enjoying Life (9:8–17)

This section is what theologians call "The Noahic Covenant." Though God spoke especially to Noah and his sons, this covenant includes all of Noah's descendants (v. 9) and "all generations to come" (v. 12 NIV). The covenant doesn't stop there, however, for it also includes every living creature (vv. 10, 12) and "all living creatures of every kind" (v. 15 NIV). Humans, birds, beasts, and wild animals are encompassed in this wonderful covenant.

In this covenant, God promised unconditionally that He would never send another flood to destroy all life on the earth. As though to make it emphatic, three times He said "never again" (vv. 11, 15 NKJV, NIV). He didn't lay down any conditions that men and women had to obey; He simply stated the fact that there would be no more universal floods. From that day on, Noah and his family could enjoy life and not worry every time the rain began to fall.

A covenant with creation. At least four times in this covenant, the Lord mentioned "every living creature." He was speaking about the animals and birds that Noah had kept safe in the ark during the flood (v. 10). Once again, we're reminded of God's special concern for animal life.

When the apostle John beheld the throne room of heaven, he saw four unusual "living creatures" worshipping before God's throne, each one having a different face (Rev. 4:6–7). The first had a face like a lion, the second like a calf, the third like a man, and the fourth like an eagle. These four faces parallel the four kinds of creatures with whom God made this covenant: wild beasts, cattle, humans, and birds (see Gen. 9:9–10). These creatures are represented perpetually before the throne of God, because the Lord is concerned about His creation. They remind us that all creation worships and praises the God who provides for His creatures and rejoices in their worship.[6]

A covenant sign. To help His people remember His covenants, God would give them a visible sign. His covenant with Abraham was sealed with the sign of circumcision (Gen. 17:11; Rom. 4:9–12), and the Mosaic Covenant at Sinai with the sign of the weekly Sabbath (Ex. 31:16–17). God's covenant with Noah and the animal creation was sealed with the sign of the rainbow. Whenever people saw the rainbow, they would remember God's promise that no future storm would ever become a worldwide flood that would destroy humanity.

Mark Twain and his friend William Dean Howells stepped out of church just as a violent rainstorm began. Howells said, "I wonder if it will stop," and Mark Twain replied, "It always has." He was right; it always has! Why? Because God made a covenant and He always keeps His word.

God spoke of the rainbow as though Noah and his family were familiar with it, so it must have existed before the flood. Rainbows are caused by the sunlight filtering through the water in the air, each drop becoming a prism to release the colors hidden in the white light of the sun. Rainbows are fragile but beautiful, and nobody has to pay to see them! Their lovely colors speak to us of what Peter called "the manifold grace of God" (1 Peter 4:10). The Greek word translated "manifold" means "various, many-colored, variegated." The rainbow reminds us of God's gracious covenant and the "many-colored" grace of God.

Let's pursue that thought. If the rainbow reminds us of God's faithfulness and grace, then why do we fret and worry? God hasn't promised that we'll never experience storms, but He has promised that the storms won't destroy us. "When you pass through the waters, I will be with you; and through the rivers, they shall not overflow you" (Isa. 43:2 NKJV). When the clouds appear and the sun is hidden, we have nothing to fear.

Let's think about the bow. A bow is an instrument of war, but God has transformed it into a picture of His grace and faithfulness, a guarantee of peace. God could certainly turn the bow of judgment upon us, because we've broken His law and deserve judgment. *But He has turned the bow toward heaven and taken the punishment for us Himself!* When Jesus died on the cross, it was the Just One suffering for the unjust (1 Peter 3:18) and bearing the suffering that rightfully belonged to us.

Rainbows are universal; you see them all over the world. God's many-colored grace is sufficient for the whole world and needs to be announced to the whole world. After all, God loves the world (John 3:16), and Christ died for the sins of the world (1 John 4:10, 14).

But the rainbow isn't only for us to see, for the Lord said, "I will look upon it" (Gen. 9:16). Certainly God doesn't forget His covenants with His people, but this is just another way of assuring us that we don't need to be afraid. When we look at the rainbow, we know that our Father is also looking at the rainbow, and therefore it becomes a bridge that brings us together.

Three rainbows. Three men in Scripture saw significant rainbows. Noah saw the rainbow *after the storm,* just as God's people see it today. But the prophet Ezekiel saw the rainbow *in the midst of the storm* when he had that remarkable vision of the wheels and the throne (Ezek. 1:28). Ezekiel also saw living creatures and each one had four faces! One was like a man, one like a lion, one like an ox, and one like an eagle—the same faces John saw (Rev. 4:6–7).

Of course, the apostle John saw the rainbow *before the storm of judgment broke loose* (v. 3). In fact, John saw a complete rainbow around the throne of God! On earth, we see "in part," but one day in heaven, we will see things fully as they really are (1 Cor. 13:12).

The personal lesson for God's people is simply this: In the storms of life, always look for the rainbow of God's covenant promise. Like John, you may see the rainbow before the storm; like Ezekiel, you may see it in the midst of the storm; or like Noah, you may have to wait until after the storm. But you will always see the rainbow of God's promise if you look by faith. That's the Old Testament version of Romans 8:28.

God's covenant with creation affects every living creature on earth.

Without it, there would be no assured continuity of nature from day to day and from season to season. We would never know when the next storm was coming and whether it would be our last.

God wants us to enjoy the blessings of natural life and spiritual life, because He "gives us richly all things to enjoy" (1 Tim. 6:17 NKJV). When you know Jesus Christ as Lord and Savior, the world of nature around you becomes much more wonderful, because the Creator has become your Father.

When in later years the American evangelist D. L. Moody talked about his conversion as a teenager, he said, "I was in a new world. The next morning the sun shone brighter and the birds sang sweeter ... the old elms waved their branches for joy, and all Nature was at peace. [It] was the most delicious joy that I had ever known."[7]

The God of creation is the God of salvation. Trust Jesus Christ and you can then truly sing, "This is my Father's world."

QUESTIONS FOR PERSONAL REFLECTION OR GROUP DISCUSSION

1. Wiersbe states that the instructions given to Noah and his family after the flood also apply to all people for all time. How can we determine which of God's instructions apply to us, not just the original recipients?

2. How does the command to "be fruitful and multiply" apply to family planning today?

3. How are children viewed in our culture?

4. What do you honestly believe is the minimum of material things that you need to function normally and to be content?

5. Why is the blood so important in the Old Testament dietary laws?

6. What is the counsel of the New Testament regarding disagreements over issues such as dietary rules?

7. How do you understand Genesis 9:6 with regard to capital punishment in our judicial system today? Are there other passages that suggest we should no longer have capital punishment?

8. We read in Genesis of God's special concern for animals and all of creation. How can you reflect God's concern?

9. The rainbow can be treated as a cliché, but what *should* we remember when we see a rainbow?

10. God is a God who makes covenant promises and sticks to them. What tempts you to doubt that? What helps you believe it?

Chapter Eleven

THE REST OF THE STORY

(Genesis 9:18—10:32)

I'm an incurable reader of biographies and autobiographies, and I've often regretted turning the page of a book and discovering a grinning skeleton lurking in the closet of someone I've admired. American columnist Russell Baker said, "The biographer's problem is that he never knows enough. The autobiographer's problem is that he knows too much."[1] But when God writes the story, He knows everything about everybody and always tells the truth, and He does it for our own good.

The history of Noah and his family now moves from rainbows to shadows, and we behold the shameful sins of a great man of faith. Dr. William Culbertson, for many years president of Moody Bible Institute in Chicago, often closed his public prayers with, "And, Lord, help us to end well." God answered that prayer for Dr. Culbertson, but not every believer now in heaven ended the race hearing God's "Well done!" (Matt. 25:21). However, let's be charitable and remember Paul's warning, "Therefore let him who thinks he stands take heed lest he fall" (1 Cor. 10:12 NKJV). After all, Noah didn't think it would happen to him!

A Family Tragedy (9:18–23)

The index for "the rest of the story" is in verses 18–19. The main characters are listed—Noah, Shem, Ham, and Japheth—and the main theme of this section is announced: how Noah's family multiplied and scattered over the earth. A contemporary reader of the Bible is tempted to skip these lists of obscure names, but that doesn't minimize their importance. These "obscure people" founded the nations that throughout Bible history interacted with each other and helped to accomplish God's purposes on this earth. The descendants of Shem—the people of Israel—have played an especially important part on the stage of history.

Disgrace (vv. 20–21). In becoming a farmer, Noah followed the vocation of his father Lamech (5:28–29). While the Bible condemns drunkenness (Prov. 20:1; 23:19–21, 29–35; Isa. 5:11; Hab. 2:15; Rom. 13:13; 1 Cor. 6:10; Eph. 5:18), it doesn't condemn the growing or eating of grapes or the drinking of wine. Grapes, raisins, and wine were important elements in the diet of Eastern peoples. In fact, in Old Testament society, wine was considered a blessing from God (Ps. 104:14–15; Deut. 14:26) and was even used with the sacrifices (Lev. 23:13; Num. 28:7).

This is the first mention of wine in Scripture, but wine-making was practiced before the flood, and Noah certainly knew what too much wine would do to him. In an attempt to exonerate Noah, some students claim that the flood brought about a change in the earth's atmosphere, and this caused the grape juice to ferment for the first time, but the defense is feeble. Noah had picked the grapes, crushed them in the winepress, put the juice into skins, and waited for the juice to ferment.

Both his drunkenness and his nakedness were disgraceful, and the two often go together (Gen. 19:30–38; Hab. 2:15–16; Lam. 4:21). Alcohol isn't a stimulant, it's a narcotic; and when the brain is affected by alcohol, the person loses self-control. At least Noah was in his own tent when this happened and not out in public. But when you consider who he was (a preacher of righteousness) and what he had done (saved his household from death), his sin becomes even more repulsive.

The Bible doesn't excuse the sins of the saints but mentions them as warnings to us not to do what they did (1 Cor. 10:6–13). As Spurgeon said, "God never allows His children to sin successfully." There's always a price to pay.

Twice Abraham lied about his wife (Gen. 12:10–20; 20:1ff.), and his son Isaac followed his bad example (26:6–16). Moses lost his temper and as a result also lost the privilege of entering the Holy Land (Num. 20:7–13). Joshua jumped to conclusions and ended up defending the enemy (Josh. 9—10). David committed adultery and arranged to have the woman's husband killed in battle (2 Sam. 11), and the sword plagued his family for years to come.

Noah didn't plan to get drunk and shamelessly expose himself, but it happened just the same. The Japanese have an appropriate proverb: "First the man takes a drink, then the drink takes a drink, and then the drink takes the man."

Disrespect (v. 22). Ham shouldn't have entered his father's tent without an invitation. Did he call to his father and receive no answer? Did he wonder if Noah was sick or perhaps even dead? Did he even know that his father had been drinking wine? These are questions the text doesn't answer, so it's useless for us to speculate. One thing is certain: Ham was disrespectful to his father in what he did.

How people respond to the sin and embarrassment of others is an indication of their character. Ham could have peeked into the tent, quickly sized up the situation, and covered his father's body, saying nothing about the incident to anyone. Instead, he seems to have enjoyed the sight and then told his two brothers about it in a rather disrespectful manner. He may even have suggested that they go take a look for themselves.

Moses hadn't yet said, "Honor your father and your mother" (Ex.

20:12 NIV), but surely the impulse is natural to children and should have been present in Ham's heart. Why would a son show such disrespect for his father? Though Ham was the youngest of the three sons, perhaps he was an Old Testament "elder brother" who was angry with his father because of something he didn't receive (Luke 15:25–32). By what he did, Ham revealed a weakness in his character that could show up in his descendants.

Decency (v. 23). Instead of laughing with Ham and going to see the humiliating sight, Shem and Japheth showed their love for their father by practicing Proverbs 10:12, "Love covers all sins" (NKJV; see 1 Peter 4:8). The brothers stood together and held a garment behind them, backed into the tent with their eyes averted, and covered Noah's naked body. "He who covers a transgression seeks love" (Prov. 17:9 NKJV), and "a prudent man covers shame" (12:16 NKJV).

Love doesn't *cleanse* sin, for only the blood of Christ can do that (1 John 1:7); nor does love *condone* sin, for love wants God's very best for others. But love does cover sin and doesn't go around exposing sin and encouraging others to spread the bad news. When people sin and we know about it, our task is to help restore them in a spirit of meekness (Gal. 6:1–2). It's been said that on the battlefield of life, Christians are prone to kick their wounded, and too often this is true. But before we condemn others, we'd better consider ourselves, for all of us are candidates for conduct unbecoming to a Christian.

A FAMILY PROPHECY (9:24–29)

When Noah awakened from his drunken stupor, he was probably ashamed of what he had done, but he was also surprised to find himself covered by a garment. Naturally, he wondered what had happened in the tent while he was asleep. The logical thing would be to speak to Japheth, his firstborn, and he and Shem must have told him what Ham had done.

These words are Noah's only recorded speech found in Scripture. It's too bad that this brief speech has been misunderstood and labeled a "curse," because what Noah said is more like a father's prophecy concerning his children and grandchildren. The word "curse" is used only once, but it's directed at Ham's youngest son Canaan and not at Ham himself. This suggests that Noah was describing the future of his sons and one grandson on the basis of what he saw in their character, not unlike what Jacob did before he died (Gen. 49).

Canaan—enslavement (v. 25). If Noah had wanted to pronounce a curse, it would have been directed at Ham, the son who had sinned against his father, but instead, he named Canaan three times. It was a principle in later Jewish law that the children could not be punished for the sins of their fathers (Deut. 24:16; Jer. 31:29–30; Ezek. 18:1–4), and it's likely that this principle applied in patriarchal times.[2]

Looking down through the centuries, Noah predicted three times that the descendants of Canaan would become the lowest of servants.[3] The Canaanites are listed in Genesis 10:15–19 and are the very nations the Israelites conquered and whose land they inhabited (15:18–21; Ex. 3:8, 17; Num. 13:29; Josh. 3:10). It's difficult to describe the moral decay of the Canaanite society, especially their religious practices, but the laws given in Leviticus 18 will give you some idea of how they lived.[4] God warned the Jews not to compromise with the Canaanite way of life and to destroy everything that would tempt them in that direction (Ex. 34:10–17; Deut. 7).

Two misconceptions should be cleared up. First, the descendants of Ham were not members of a black race but were Caucasian, so there's no basis in this so-called "curse of Canaan" for the institution of slavery. Second, in spite of their evil ways, some of these Hamitic peoples built large and advanced civilizations, including the Babylonians, Assyrians, and Egyptians. In one sense, we can say that the descendants of Ham "served" the whole world through the ideas and implements that they discovered and developed. Like the Cainites (Gen. 4:17–24), these nations were gifted at creating things for this world (Luke 16:8).

Shem—enrichment (v. 26). Noah didn't bless Shem; he blessed "the Lord, the God of Shem" (NIV). In so doing, Noah gave glory to God for what He will do with the descendants of Shem. Noah acknowledged before his sons that whatever Shem possessed would be God's gift, and whatever blessing Shem brought to the world in the future would be because of the grace of God.

Shem, of course, is the ancestor of Abraham (11:10–32) who is the founder of the Hebrew nation; so Noah was talking about the Jewish people. That the Lord would enrich the Jewish people spiritually was promised to Abraham (12:1–3) and later explained by Paul (Rom. 3:1–4; 9:1–13). It's through Israel that we have the knowledge of the true God, the written Word of God, and the Savior, Jesus Christ, who was born in Bethlehem of the tribe of Judah. In the Hebrew, "Shem" means "name," and it's the people of Israel who have preserved the name of the Lord.

Shem was Noah's second-born son (Gen. 9:24; 10:21), but wherever the three sons are listed, Shem's name is first (5:32; 6:10; 9:18; 10:1; 1 Chron. 1:4). It's another instance in Genesis of the grace of God elevating the second-born to the place of the firstborn. God chose Abel instead of Cain (Gen. 4:4–5), Isaac instead of Ishmael (17:15–22), and Jacob instead of Esau (25:19–23). Paul discusses this profound theological truth in Romans 9.

Japheth—enlargement (v. 27). He was the ancestor of what we generally call the "Gentile nations." We have here a play on words, for in the Hebrew the name Japheth is very close to the word that means "to enlarge." The Hamites built large civilizations in the east, and the Semites settled in the land of Canaan and surrounding territory, but the descendants of Japheth spread out much farther than their relatives and even reached what we know as Asia Minor and Europe. They were a people who would multiply and move into new territory.

However, while the descendants of Japheth were successful in their conquests, when it came to things spiritual, they would have to depend on Shem. God is the God of Shem and the descendants of Japheth would find God "in the tents of Shem." Israel was chosen by God to be a "light to the Gentiles" (Isa. 42:6; 49:6), for "salvation is of the Jews" (John 4:22). Sad to say, for the most part, the nation of Israel failed to witness to the Gentiles that they might believe in the true and living God (Isa. 52:5; Rom. 2:24).

When Jesus came to earth, He brought light to the Gentiles (Luke 2:32), and the apostles and the early church carried that light to the nations (Acts 1:8; 13:47). The descendants of Noah's three sons were represented in the early church: the Ethiopian treasurer, a descendant of Ham (8:26ff.);[5] Paul, a descendant of Shem (Acts 9); and Cornelius and his family, who were descendants of Japheth (Acts 10).

Noah lived another three-and-a-half centuries, and we have every reason to believe that he walked with God and served Him faithfully. As far as the record is concerned, he fell once, and certainly he repented and the Lord forgave him. In our walk with God, we climb the hills and sometimes we descend into the valleys. As Alexander Whyte used to say, "The victorious Christian life is a series of new beginnings."

A FAMILY LEGACY (10:1–32)

This chapter is known as "The Table of Nations" and is unique in the annals of ancient history. The purpose of the chapter is given at the beginning (v. 1) and the end (v. 32): to explain how the earth was repopulated after the flood by the descendants of the three sons of Noah. You find a similar (but not identical) listing in 1 Chronicles 1.

Caution! Before we look at some of the details of this chapter, and then try to draw some spiritual lessons from it, we need to heed some warnings.

First, the listing is not a typical genealogy that gives only the names of descendants. The writer reminds us that these ancient peoples had their own "clans and languages … territories and nations" (Gen. 10:31 NIV). In other words, this is a genealogy plus an atlas plus a history book. We're watching the movements of people and nations in the ancient world.

Second, the listing isn't complete. For example, we don't find Edom, Moab, and Ammon mentioned, and yet these were important nations in biblical history. The fact that there are seventy nations in the list suggests that the arrangement may be deliberately artificial, an approach often used in writing such listings.[6] There were seventy persons in Jacob's family when they went to Egypt (Gen. 46:27; Ex. 1:5), and our Lord sent approximately seventy disciples out to preach the Word (Luke 10:1).

Third, it's difficult to identify some of these nations and give them "modern" names. Over the centuries, nations can change their names, move to different locations, modify their language, and even alter their racial composition through intermarriage.

Japheth's descendants (vv. 2–5). Seven sons are named and seven grandsons from only two of the sons. Does this mean that the other five sons had no children born to them, or is it another evidence of the selective approach of the compiler? Japheth is the ancestor of the Gentile nations who located north and west of the land of Canaan. These would be the distant nations, the countries that represented the "outer limits" of civilization for the average Old Testament Jew (Ps. 72:8–10).

Ham's descendants (vv. 6–20). Cush is ancient Ethiopia (not the modern nation), Mizraim is Egypt, and Put may be Libya. We've already touched upon the peoples of Canaan. The descendants of Ham located in areas we'd identify today as Egypt, Palestine, the Sudan, Saudi Arabia, and Yemen.

At this point in the listing there's a "parenthesis" to discuss a famous man, Nimrod, the founder of a great empire (vv. 8–12). He's mentioned because the nations he founded played an important part in the history of Israel, and also because one of them (Babel) is discussed in the next section of Genesis.

In the *King James Version,* Nimrod is called "a mighty one in the earth" and "a mighty hunter before the Lord" (vv. 8–9). The word translated "mighty" refers to a champion, somebody who is superior in strength and courage. It's translated "mighty men" in 1 Kings 1:8 and 10 and refers to David's special bodyguards. The image of Nimrod in the text isn't that of a sportsman hunting game[7] but rather of a tyrant ruthlessly conquering men and establishing an empire. He built four cities in Shinar (Babylonia) and four more in Assyria. Both Babylon and Assyria became the enemies of Israel and were used of God to chasten His disobedient people. We'll learn more about Babylon in the next study.

Shem's descendants (vv. 21–31). Shem is usually mentioned first, but he's listed last this time so that the narrative can move right into the story of Babel and the genealogy of Abraham, who descended from Shem (11:10ff.). Five sons are mentioned, but the emphasis is on the family of Arphaxad because he was the grandfather of Eber (10:24). Abraham, the father of the Hebrew nation, came from the line of Eber, and his story begins in chapter 12.[8]

There's another "parenthesis" in 10:25 to discuss the "dividing of the earth" during the days of Peleg, which means "division." This is probably referring to the dividing and dispersing of the nations described in chapter 11. However, some students think this "division" refers to a special dividing of the continents and rearranging of the landmasses.[9]

Significance. This list of names and places carries with it some important theological truths, not the least of which is that *Jehovah God is the Lord of the nations.* God gave the nations their inheritance (Deut. 32:8) and "determined the times before appointed, and the bounds of their habitation" (Acts 17:26). In spite of despots like Nimrod, Jehovah is the God of geography and of history; He is in control. What God promises, He performs, and Noah's prophecy about his sons came true.

Second, in spite of external differences, *all nations belong to the same human family.* God made us all "of one blood" (Acts 17:26), and no race or people can claim to be superior to any other race or people. While in His providence, God has permitted some nations to make greater progress economically and politically than other nations, their achievements don't prove that they are better than others (Prov. 22:2).

Third, *God has a purpose for the nations to fulfill.* The account in Genesis 9:24—11:32 makes it clear that God's chosen nation was Israel. From chapter 12 on, Israel will be center stage in the narrative. But God also used Egypt, Babylon, Assyria, Media-Persia, and Rome to accomplish His purposes with reference to the Jewish people. God can use pagan rulers like Nebuchadnezzar, Cyrus, Darius, and even Augustus Caesar.

Fourth, *God is concerned for all the nations.* Frequently in the book of Psalms you find the phrase "all ye lands" or "all nations." Psalms 66:1–8 and 67 both express this universal vision that all the nations of the earth come to know God and serve Him. The church's commission to go into all the world isn't a New Testament afterthought; it's written into the warp and woof of the Old Testament story.

Finally, what's written in Genesis 9—10 must have been an encouragement to the people of Israel when they conquered Canaan. They knew that they were the chosen people of God and that the Canaanites would be their servants. They also knew that their God was the Lord of the nations and could dispose of them as He pleased. The conquest of Canaan was a victory of faith in God's promises, which explains why God admonished Joshua to meditate on the Word of God (Josh. 1:8).

Noah's three sons left a mixed legacy to the world, but the Lord of the nations was still in charge, and history is still His story.[10]

QUESTIONS FOR PERSONAL REFLECTION
OR GROUP DISCUSSION

1. We all want "to end well," as Dr. Culbertson prayed. What can we do now and in the future to be sure "to end well"?

2. What lessons can we learn from reading about the sins and failures of the saints in the Bible?

3. Recall two incidents when you have seen a right and a wrong response to the sin and embarrassment of others. What does this indicate about the character of those responding?

4. What does Galatians 6:1–2 say about what to do when people sin and we know about it?

5. Noah's only recorded speech is sometimes viewed as a curse and sometimes as a prophecy. What difference would this make?

6. Christians have previously used the passage about Canaan being a servant of others to justify their enslavement of African Americans. What can we learn about biblical interpretation from this grave error?

7. If, as Alexander Whyte said, "the victorious Christian life is a series of new beginnings," in what circumstances could you share this as a comfort to others?

8. What do we need to remember as we read genealogies in the Bible?

9. Since Jehovah is "the God of geography and of history," does this mean that God is behind all the political disputes, coups, and tribal slaughter?

10. In what manner are children sometimes punished for their parents' sins?

Chapter Twelve

CAUTION—GOD AT WORK

(Genesis 11)

Man proposes, but God disposes."

That familiar statement is almost a religious cliché. Many people who use it don't even know what it means. It was written by the Augustinian monk Thomas à Kempis (ca. 1380–1471) in his classic book *On the Imitation of Christ.* An expanded version is the proverb, "Man does what he can, God does what He will." Solomon used more words but said it best: "There are many plans in a man's heart, nevertheless the Lord's counsel—that will stand" (Prov. 19:21 NKJV).

Few chapters in the Bible illustrate this truth better than Genesis 11. When you read the narrative about Babel and then read the genealogies that follow, your immediate impression is that God is at work in His world and is accomplishing His purposes in spite of the plans and projects of sinful people.

GOD STOPS A REVOLT (11:1–9)

Four great events are recorded in Genesis 1—11: the creation of the universe, the fall of man, the flood, and the attempted construction of the

Tower of Babel. These chapters reveal that where mankind disobeys God, the Lord judges sin, and then in His grace makes a new beginning.

Adam and Eve sinned, but God clothed them and promised to send the world a Redeemer. Cain killed Abel, but God sent Seth to carry on the godly line. The Sethites intermarried with the godless Cainites, and God had to wipe the earth clean with a flood, but Noah and his family believed God's Word and were spared. After the flood, the descendants of Noah's three sons repopulated the earth. But the new beginning with Noah eventually led to one of the most arrogant revolts against God recorded anywhere in Scripture.

Rebellion (vv. 1–4). It's likely that the events in chapter 11 occurred prior to those in chapter 10 and that the scattering described in chapter 10 was the consequence of God's judgment at Babel. Perhaps the story was placed here in Genesis so it could lead into the genealogy of Shem which leads into the genealogy of Abraham, the founder of the Hebrew nation. The arrangement, then, is literary and not chronological.

God had commanded the peoples to be fruitful and multiply and to scatter across the earth, but they decided to move to Nimrod's city of Babylon and settle there (11:1–12). This move was blatant rebellion against God's command that the people scatter. Apparently Nimrod wanted them in his cities and under his control.

The "tower" that they built at Babel was what is known as a "ziggurat." Archeologists have excavated several of these large structures which were built primarily for religious purposes. A ziggurat was like a pyramid except that the successive levels were recessed so that you could walk to the top on "steps." At the top was a special shrine dedicated to a god or goddess. In building the structure, the people weren't trying to climb up to heaven to dethrone God; rather, they hoped that the god or goddess they worshipped would come down from heaven to meet them. The structure and the city were called "Babel," which means "the gate of the gods."

This infamous project was an arrogant declaration of war against the Lord, not unlike the revolt described in Psalm 2:1–3. To begin with, the people were resisting God's edict to scatter and repopulate the earth. Motivated perhaps by fear as well as pride, they decided to build a city and a great ziggurat and stay together. But even more, they wanted to make a name for themselves so that others would admire them and perhaps come and join them. Their purpose statement was the Devil's lie in Eden: "You will be like God" (Gen. 3:5 NIV).

The people had several things in their favor. They were truly a "united nations," one people (11:6) speaking one language and using one vocabulary and dictionary.[1] They were motivated by one spirit of pride and one compelling desire to make a name for themselves. The only thing missing was the approval of God.

God's response (vv. 5–9). "Whom the gods would destroy," wrote historian Charles Beard, "they first make mad with power."[2] From Babel to Belshazzar (Dan. 5), and from Herod (Acts 12:20–25) to Hitler, God has demonstrated repeatedly that it doesn't pay to rebel against His will. "Pride goes before destruction, and a haughty spirit before a fall" (Prov. 16:18 NKJV), and Jesus warned that those who exalt themselves will be abased (Matt. 23:12).

God in heaven is never perplexed or paralyzed by what people do on earth. Babel's conceited "Let's go up!" was answered by heaven's calm "Let's go down!" "He who sits in the heavens shall laugh; the Lord shall hold them in derision" (Ps. 2:4 NKJV). Of course, God doesn't have to investigate to know what's going on in His universe; the language is used only to dramatize God's intervention.

As with Adam and Eve in the garden (Gen. 3:22–24), God's judgment at Babel not only dealt with the immediate sins but also helped to prevent future problems. The unity of mankind would only give people a false sense of power that would lead them into even greater rebellion against

God. By confusing their language and scattering them over all the earth, God graciously spared their lives and gave them opportunity to return to Him. He could have destroyed the builders, their city, and their tower, but He chose to let them live.

The word "babel" sounds like the Hebrew word *balal* which means "confusion." Because of God's judgment, the "gate of the gods" became the "the door to confusion." Instead of making a name for themselves, God gave the project a new name! In His church, "God is not the author of confusion" (1 Cor. 14:33), but in the world, God sometimes uses confusion to humble people and keep them from uniting against His will.

The word "Shem" means "name" in Hebrew, and Abraham, a descendant of Shem, was promised that God would make his name great (Gen. 12:2). The people of the world depend on their own wisdom and efforts, and yet they fail to achieve lasting fame. Who knows the name of anybody who worked on the famous Tower of Babel? Yet the name of Abraham is known around the world and revered by Jews, Muslims, and Christians. There's a vast difference between mankind's "We will make our name great!" and God's "I will make your name great!"

The book of Genesis emphasizes names; and in this book, God changes several names. For example, Abram becomes Abraham, Sarai becomes Sarah, Esau becomes Edom, Jacob becomes Israel, and so on. What God calls a thing is far more important than what we call it. When He was creating the world, God gave names to things; He even asked Adam to name the animals. The word "babel" would convey "gates of the gods" to very few people today; most of them would think "confusion."

Our reply. The story of Babel isn't just a part of ancient history, because Babel and Babylon present a spiritual challenge to every believer today.

Babylon eventually became a great city and a great empire. In 606–586 BC, the Babylonian armies attacked and captured the kingdom of Judah, burned the temple and the city of Jerusalem, and took thousands of Jews captive to Babylon for seventy years. God used the cruel and idolatrous Babylonians to chasten His own disobedient people.

But in Scripture, Babylon symbolizes worldly pride, moral corruption, and defiance against God. The biblical contrast is between the earthly city of Babylon that rebels against God, and the heavenly city of Jerusalem that brings glory to God. You will want to read Jeremiah 50—51 and Revelation 17—19 to appreciate the contrasts between these two cities. Babylon represents the world system that opposes God, hates Jesus Christ, and appeals to the baser appetites of human nature. Babylon is the opposite of the heavenly Jerusalem which is the city of the saints (Heb. 12:18ff.).

In the original Babel, the people wanted to build a tower that reached up to heaven, but in the Babylon of Revelation 17—18, Babylon's sins reach up to heaven (18:5). The original worldwide unity that Nimrod desired for the Genesis Babylon will one day be achieved by Satan's godless world system (17:3, 9, 11, 23). Earthly Babylon is called a prostitute, while the Holy City from heaven is called bride of Christ (17:1–2; 21:9ff.).

"Every generation builds its own towers," writes psychotherapist Naomi H. Rosenblatt, and she is right.[3] Whether these are actual skyscrapers (the Willis Tower [formerly Sears] and Tribune Tower in Chicago, the Eiffel Tower in Paris, the Trump Tower in New York City), or megacorporations that circle the globe, the idea is the same: "We will make a name for ourselves." God's people can't escape being in the world, because it's in the world that we have our ministry, but we must avoid being of the world. We're not here to build the arrogant towers of men; we're here to help build the church of Jesus Christ.[4]

What humanity can't achieve by means of its "proud towers," Jesus Christ has achieved by dying on a humiliating cross. All who trust Jesus Christ are one in Him (Gal. 3:27) and will share heaven together, regardless of race, nation, language, or tribe (Rev. 7:9). While the world system is outwardly producing uniformity, inwardly it's tearing things apart. What social scientists are now calling "technopoly" is controlling people's lives.[5]

But the Holy Spirit is using the church as an agent of reconciliation to bring people together in Jesus Christ (Eph. 1:10; 2 Cor. 5:14–21). In one sense, Pentecost was a reversal of Babel, for the people present in Jerusalem at Pentecost heard the praises of God in their own languages (Acts 2:1–12). The day will come when people from every tribe and nation will worship Jesus Christ (Rev. 15:4) and the judgment of Babel will be done away (Zeph. 3:9).

Each person must make a choice. Will we identify with Babylon or Jerusalem, the worldly prostitute or the heavenly bride?

GOD SUSTAINS A FAMILY (11:10–26)

God had promised that He would send a Redeemer, the seed of the woman (3:15), who would defeat Satan and bring salvation. Noah's prophecy revealed that God would bless the world through the line of Shem, the "Semites" who were the ancestors of the Hebrew people (9:26–27). "Shem was the ancestor of all the sons of Eber" (10:21 NIV), and it's likely that the word "Hebrew" comes from the name "Eber."

Genesis gives us two genealogies of Shem, in 10:21–29 and in 11:10–26. The first genealogy lists all five of his sons and five of his grandsons, but then it focuses on the descendants of Arphaxad: Shelah, Eber, and Eber's two sons Peleg and Joktan. It lists Joktan's many sons but ignores Peleg's descendants. But the genealogy in chapter 11 picks up Peleg's side of the family and takes us through to Abraham. The genealogy in Genesis 5 takes us from Adam to Noah, and the one in Genesis 11 goes from Noah's son Shem to Terah and his son Abraham.

Except that both lists have ten generations, the listing in 11:10–26 is different from the genealogy in Genesis 5. For one thing, it doesn't contain the repeated phrase "and he died." The emphasis is on how old the man was at the birth of his firstborn son. The people named in 11:10–26 didn't live as long as the men named in Genesis 5. The list begins with Noah's 950 years and dwindles down to Nahor's 148 years. The post-flood generations were starting to feel the physical consequences of sin in the human body.

The important thing about this genealogy is that it records the faithfulness of God in watching over His people and fulfilling His promises. What to us is only a list of names was to God a "bridge" from the appointment of Shem to the call of Abraham. God has deigned to use people to help accomplish His will on earth, and people are fragile and not always obedient. But the "bridge" was built and the covenant promises sustained.

GOD STARTS A NATION (11:27–32)

If Genesis 1—11 is a record of four key events—creation, the fall, the flood, and the judgment at Babel—then Genesis 12—50 is the record of the lives of four key men: Abraham, Isaac, Jacob, and Joseph. In this paragraph, five persons stand out: Abraham and his wife Sarah;[6] Terah, Abraham's father; and Nahor and Haran, Abraham's brothers. Haran died and left his son Lot behind.

It was God's purpose to call a man and his wife and from them build a family. From that family He would build a nation, and from that nation, God would bless all the nations of the earth (12:1–3; 18:18). From start to finish, it was a work of God's grace; for when God called Abraham and Sarah, they belonged to a family that worshipped idols (Josh. 24:2). In both Ur of the Chaldees and Haran, the people worshipped the moon god.

According to Stephen (Acts 7:2), "the God of glory" appeared to Abraham and called him to go to Canaan. Abraham must have shared this amazing message with his family and told them that he and Sarah were leaving. He was supposed to take only Sarah and depart, leaving his family behind (Gen. 12:1); but everybody went with him except his brother Nahor and, of course, his brother Haran who had died. Nahor and his wife Milcah will show up again later in the story (22:20), but Nahor *was the man who stayed.* Even though he remained in idolatrous Ur of the

Chaldees, did Nahor believe the message his brother gave him about the true God of glory? We hope he did.

It appears that Terah did believe and took charge of the family and their travels (11:31), but Terah *was the man who stopped.* He traveled 500 miles, as far as the city of Haran, and there he settled down and there he died. Perhaps the journey was too great for him, but it was God's plan that Abraham and Sarah follow Him without their family. The death of Terah left them only with Lot, the son of Haran who had died back in Ur. Lot *became the man who strayed,* because he finally left Abraham and settled down in the wicked city of Sodom (13:10–13; 14:12; 19:1ff.).

The remarkable thing about God's call of Abraham and Sarah was that they were childless. Abram means "exalted father," but he wasn't a father at all! They were the least likely candidates to have a family and build a great nation. But God's ways are not our ways (Isa. 55:8–9), and by calling and blessing a barren couple, the Lord revealed the greatness of His power and His glory. Abram would be named "Abraham," which means "father of many nations."

There's quite a contrast between man's ways at Babel and God's ways in calling Abraham and Sarah. The world depends on large numbers of powerful people in order to accomplish things, but God chose two weak people and started a new nation. The people at Babel wanted to make a name for themselves, but God promised to make Abraham's name great. The workers at Babel followed the wisdom of this world, but Abraham and Sarah trusted the Word of God (Heb. 11:11–12). Babel was built by the energy of the flesh and the motivation of pride, but the nation of Israel was built by the grace and power of God and in spite of human weakness.

We live in a confused world and Babel is still with us. But God still has His faithful remnant that follows Him by faith and keeps their eyes on the heavenly city (vv. 13–16).

Are you a part of that remnant?

QUESTIONS FOR PERSONAL REFLECTION
OR GROUP DISCUSSION

1. What does this mean: "Man proposes, but God disposes"?

2. As we read about the cycles of disobedience, judgment, and new beginnings, what do we learn about God's character?

3. What was the goal of building the Tower of Babel?

4. What were the positive and negative elements of the unity at Babel?

5. How does God use both confusion and unity? How might Satan use them?

6. When you daydream, in what ways do you dream of making a name for yourself? How is your local church tempted to make a name for itself?

7. How can we tell the difference between godly ambition and selfish ambition?

8. Why do you think the lifespan of humans became shorter? (See Gen. 6:3.)

9. God called an idol-worshipping, barren couple to build His nation. What hope can we find in this?

10. How can Christians use global technology and power in a right way? What are the dangers to avoid?

Chapter Thirteen

BACK TO BASICS

(Review of Genesis 1—11)

What the foundation is to the house, what the Constitution is to United States law, and what the periodic table of elements is to chemistry, the book of Genesis is to the Bible. It's basic. An understanding of the basic truths of Genesis, especially chapters 1—11, will give you the key you need to unlock the rest of Scripture and to live to the glory of God. But you don't stop with Genesis 1—11; you build on it.

Let's review some of these basics.

GOD IS REAL AND WE CAN TRUST HIM

The Bible opens with a declaration that God exists: "In the beginning God" (1:1). Genesis presents no philosophical arguments to prove God's existence; it just puts Him at the beginning of everything. When you open your Bible, God is there, and He[1] was there before the Bible was written or even the universe was created.

The God you meet in Genesis 1—11 is not only eternal, but He's also wise and powerful. He is a great God, and so great is His power that He only has to speak to make things happen. And so great is His wisdom that what He creates is to be—and it works! From the tiniest one-celled animal to the biggest galaxy, in all creation God's power and wisdom are manifested.

And yet this great God is a personal God. He pays attention to us and wants to be our Lord and our Friend!

He is a holy God who will not condone sin. He judged the personal sins of Adam, Eve, and Cain, and also the corporate sins of the antediluvian population and the people at Babel. But at the same time, He is a God of love who created us in His image and longs to fellowship with us and reveal Himself to us. Our sins grieve Him, but in His grace, He forgives those who trust Him and will give them another chance.

The God of Genesis has a plan for mankind. He promised to send a Redeemer who would conquer Satan and bring salvation for the human race (3:15). He fulfilled that promise in sending Jesus Christ, the Son of God, to die on the cross for the sins of the world. You don't really know God until you have trusted Jesus Christ to save you from your sins.

WE LIVE IN GOD'S CREATION

The universe was created by God, not by chance. He made everything and He keeps everything going. The universe is not an accident. It's the incredible masterpiece of a wise and powerful God who works everything according to the counsel of His own perfect will.

The complexity of the universe reveals the power and wisdom of God, and the beauty of the universe shows His love. He could have made a dull world, but He decorated His world with a riot of color and gave us a variety of plants, animals, and people to enjoy. Day after day and night after night, creation reveals the glory of God (Ps. 19).

Because this is God's creation, we're but stewards of what He's given us. We must use the wealth of creation for the good of others and the glory of God, remembering that one day we'll give God an accounting of our stewardship. To waste or exploit the wealth of creation, or heedlessly mar the beauty of creation, is to sin against God. It's not just a matter of ecology; it's a matter of theology: This is our Father's world.

God generously gives to us "richly all things to enjoy" (1 Tim. 6:17), and we should thank Him for His gifts and use them wisely.

WE ARE MADE IN THE IMAGE OF GOD

Men and women are created, not evolved, and they're created in the image of God. This is a tremendous privilege and a great responsibility. Every baby that's conceived is made in God's image and has the right to live, to be in a loving family, to come to know God through Jesus Christ, and to enjoy a life that's purposeful and fulfilling.

Since God has given us a mind to think with, we need to read His Word and learn His truth. He's given us a will to decide with, and we must make wise decisions that please Him. We have hearts to love Him, and we show this love by fellowshipping with Him and obeying His will. Our inner being is spiritual, and we need God dwelling within if we're to have inner peace and satisfaction. "Thou hast made us for Thyself," wrote Augustine, "and our hearts are restless until they rest in Thee."

The fact that we're all created in the image of God means that we must love and protect one another. God gives life and only God can take it away. He's given to human government the authority for capital punishment, for the murderer attacks the very image of God.

The image of God in us has been marred by sin, but that image can be restored as we walk with God and yield to His Spirit (2 Cor. 3:18). Since God made us, He knows what's best for us, and He's given us His Word as our guidebook for life. It's the "manual of operations," and we must get acquainted with it. When all else fails, read the instructions.

OBEDIENCE IS THE KEY TO USEFULNESS, JOY, AND BLESSING

Our first parents disobeyed God's Word and plunged the entire human race into sin. Cain disobeyed and became a wanderer. Noah obeyed and God saved him and his family from destruction and blessed them after the flood was over. Whenever we disobey God, we break our communion with Him and lose the joy of His presence. Obedience is the key to blessing; disobedience is the way to unhappiness and chastening.

Satan Is Real, but Is a Defeated Enemy

Satan is not eternal; he's a created being. He's not all-knowing, all-powerful, or present in all places at all times. He's limited, but he wants you to think he's as great as God and worthy of your obedience. Satan is very powerful and very subtle, and in ourselves we're no match for him.

Satan wants to be god in our lives; he wants our worship and our service. He tempts us by questioning God's Word: "Has God really said?" He promises to make us like God, but he never keeps that promise. The first step in victory over Satan is not to listen to his offers or believe his promises. We need to know and believe God's truth if we want to detect and defeat the Devil's lies.

Satan has been defeated by Jesus Christ, and through Christ we can claim victory (Col. 2:15; Rom. 16:20; 1 Cor. 10:13).

There Is Such a Thing As Sin

The world may call it a blunder, a mistake, a weakness, or an accident, but if it's disobedience to God's will, God calls it sin. Sin is serious because it leads to death and judgment. Like any loving father, God is grieved when His children sin, and God judges sin. But God also forgives and provides the cleansing that we need.

When we sin, our tendency is to run away and try to hide, but this is the worst thing we can do. You can't hide from God. The only thing to do is to repent, confess, and claim His forgiveness. God does give us another opportunity to obey Him and be blessed.

Sex Is God's Idea and He Knows Best
How It Should Be Used

God made the first humans "male and female." He did it not just so they could reproduce and keep the human race going, but also that they might learn to love and enjoy one another and discover their loving relationship to the Lord. His original intent was one man for one woman for one lifetime.

The Bible isn't a "sex manual," but it does make some things very clear. It's clear that sexual sins are destructive not only to the body and the inner person, but also to other people, especially one's mate and family. God created man and woman for each other; any other combination is out of God's will, no matter what society and the courts might say. God invented marriage, and sex outside the loving bonds of marriage is wrong.

All Humans Are Made of One Blood

God separated the descendants of Noah into various tongues and nations, but they are all the sons and daughters of Adam and Eve. By the providence of God, some nations and races have made more rapid progress in this world than have others, but this doesn't mean these progressive nations are better than other people. We are of one blood, and no race can claim to be superior to another race.

God has ordained that men and women shall work. Work isn't a form of punishment; rather, it's an opportunity to cooperate with God in caring for His creation.

Israel Is God's Chosen People

This doesn't mean that they're better than others, but only that they have God's call upon them and therefore have a greater responsibility in this world. God chose them because He loved them, not because of their intrinsic worth (Deut. 7:6–11). God called Israel to bring blessing to the whole world, and because of Israel, we have the knowledge of the true God, the written Word of God, and most of all, the Savior Jesus Christ. No Christian should be guilty of anti-Semitism in thought, word, or deed.

God Doesn't Change and Is Always in Control

God is still on the throne and always knows what He's doing. He's long-suffering toward sinners, but eventually He judges sin and rewards the righteous. Whether it's the farthest star or the most minute atom, God knows where everything is and what everything is doing; and everything He's made will ultimately accomplish His will on this earth.

God has built laws into this universe which, if we obey them, work for us, but if we disobey them, they work against us. Science is simply thinking God's thoughts after Him, discovering these laws and putting them to work. The Creator has the right to "break" His own laws and do the miraculous.

Our Relationship to God Is Based on Faith

"But without faith it is impossible to please Him, for he who comes to God must believe that He is, and that He is a rewarder of those who diligently seek him" (Heb. 11:6 NKJV).

We live on promises, not explanations.

Living for God Is the Most Rewarding Life Possible

God has a different purpose for each of us to fulfill, and He enables us to fulfill it as we trust His Word and obey His will. Whatever He calls us to do can be done to the glory of God. While there are times when it seems like the righteous are suffering and the wicked are succeeding, in the end, the righteous will get their eternal reward and the wicked their eternal punishment.

The Christian life isn't always the easiest life, but it is the most satisfying and rewarding life.

These are just a few of the basics found in Genesis 1—11, and illustrated and explained in the rest of the Bible. When you give your life to Christ and build on these basic truths, you build on a solid foundation that can't be moved. To ignore these basics is to build on the sand and make a life that won't survive the storms of life or the final judgment from God. Jesus calls us all back to the basics. Read and ponder Matthew 7:21–27.

QUESTIONS FOR PERSONAL REFLECTION
OR GROUP DISCUSSION

1. Why do you think God's revelation of Himself didn't include philosophical arguments to prove His existence?

2. What attributes of God do you see displayed in Genesis 1—11?

3. When we hear ecology and "save the earth" messages, what must Christians add?

4. What are some implications of the fact that all persons are made in the image of God?

5. What is the key to receiving blessing from God? What are the consequences of disobedience?

6. How does your thinking about Satan compare with what the Bible teaches? How can we have victory over Satan?

7. What are God's purposes for sex and marriage?

8. In comparing different races of humans, how are we all alike? How are we all different?

9. If you were to be given a tremendous amount of faith today, what do you think you'd be inspired to try?

10. What is God calling you to do? How will you be able to accomplish it?

NOTES

A Word from the Author

1. *Be Basic* is the first volume in the "BE" series covering Genesis. See also *Be Obedient* (Gen. 12—25) and *Be Authentic* (Gen. 25—50).

2. That Moses could write (Acts 7:22) and kept a record of important events is stated in Exodus 17:14; 24:4; Numbers 33:1–2; Deuteronomy 31:9; and Joshua 1:8. Both Scripture and Jewish tradition point to Moses as the author of the Pentateuch, the first five books of the Old Testament (Josh. 8:31; 23:6; 2 Kings 14:6; 2 Chron. 25:4; 35:12; Ezra 6:18; Neh. 8:1; 13:1). When Jesus referred to or quoted from the Pentateuch, He connected these books with Moses (Matt. 19:8; Mark 10:3; Luke 20:37; John 5:45–46).

Chapter One

1. It's doubtful that the ancient theologians ever asked this particular question, but the topic isn't totally irrelevant. Angels are spirits and have no physical bodies, except temporarily when sent on special missions; so how do they occupy space? Thomas Aquinas discussed the matter in his *Summa Theologica,* so the question is important.

2. A. W. Tozer, *The Knowledge of the Holy* (New York: Harper and Brothers, 1961), 39.

3. Of course, every human being will exist forever, either in heaven or hell, but as far as this world is concerned, we're all strangers and pilgrims only passing through.

4. "Lonely" doesn't suggest that God needed friends. The word means "solitary."

5. A. W. Tozer, *The Christian Book of Mystical Verse* (Harrisburg, PA: Christian Publications, 1963), 7.

6. In our day, "process theology" grew out of the teachings of the British philosopher Alfred North Whitehead (1861–1947), and his

disciple Charles Hartshorne gave it wide exposure. Process theology was popularized by Rabbi Harold S. Kushner in his book *When Bad Things Happen to Good People*. Kushner claimed that God was too weak now to do anything about cancer, war, and the tragedies of life; but as we trust Him and do good, we strengthen Him to do better. For the evangelical point of view, see *Process Theology* edited by Ronald H. Nash (Baker Book House, 1987), and my book *Why Us? When Bad Things Happen to God's People* (Fleming H. Revell, 1984).

7. The conjunction "and" in the Christian baptismal formula is important, for it shows the equality of the Persons of the Godhead.

8. The doctrine of divine election is not an excuse to not share the gospel with others. The same God who ordained the end—the salvation of the lost—has also ordained the means to the end, which is the witness of His people and their prayers for success for His Word. God chooses people to salvation and then calls them by His gospel (2 Thess. 2:13–14). The two go together. We don't know who the elect are, and we have been ordered to take the gospel to the whole world (Mark 16:15; Acts 1:8).

9. Dr. H. A. Ironside, for eighteen years pastor of Chicago's Moody Church, used to illustrate this truth by describing a door, over which hung a sign that read, "Whosoever will may come." Believing that, you walked through the door and were saved. Then you looked back and read another sign hanging over the inside of the door: "Chosen in Christ before the foundation of the world."

10. These chapter divisions are arbitrary since there is an overlapping of generations in the narratives as there always is in human history. Technically, the "generations of Jacob" begins at 37:2, but Jacob's story starts much earlier and moves Isaac into the background. There is no section labeled "the generations of Joseph" since Joseph is a part of the Jacob narrative which closes the book of Genesis.

11. See Morgan's *The Analyzed Bible* and *Living Messages of the Books of the Bible,* both published by Fleming H. Revell.

Chapter Two

1. Richard M. Nixon, *In the Arena* (New York: Simon and Schuster, 1990), 206.

2. John describes seven days in the life of Jesus (John 1:19–28, 29–34, 35–42, 43–51; 2:1), obviously a parallel to Genesis 1. Moses wrote of the old creation but John of the new creation (2 Cor. 5:17).

3. The Hebrew word *bara* means "to initiate something new, to bring into existence." It's used in the creation account to describe the creation of sea creatures and fowl (Gen. 1:21), the creation of man and woman (v. 27), and the whole work of creation (1; 2:3–4).

4. The "gap theory," stated in G. H. Pember's book, *Earth's Earliest Ages,* and popularized by the *Scofield Reference Bible,* affirms that the original creation of Genesis 1:1 was judged when Satan fell, and that verses 3ff. describe a remaking of the ruined creation. Verse 2 should read, "And the earth became without form and void." Hence, there was a "gap" of unknown duration between the first two verses of Genesis. But why would God ruin the whole creation just because of Satan's rebellion? And if He created it instantly, why would He take six days to restore it? There are capable defenders of both views, and they all claim that the Hebrew text is on their side. To me, it appears that verses 3ff. are describing God's original acts of creation and that we don't have to put a "gap" between verse 1 and verse 2 in order to solve any problems.

5. The image in verse 2 is that of the eagle hovering over its young (Deut. 32:11). In both the Hebrew *(ruah)* and the Greek *(pneuma),* the word for "Spirit" also means "wind" (see John 3:8), so the verse could be translated "and God's wind swept across the waters." However, "Spirit" seems to be the logical translation.

6. "Without form, and void" is the Hebrew phrase *tohu wabohu,* which describes utter waste, vanity, and ruin. Jeremiah borrowed the image to describe God's judgment of the land of Judah (Jer. 4:23), and Isaiah used it to describe the ruin of Edom.

7. Some commentators believe that God's work on the fourth day was not to *create* the luminaries but *to assign them their tasks.* However, the description in Genesis 1:14–19 parallels that of the other five days and gives every evidence of explaining the creative act of God.

8. When speaking of a twenty-four hour day, the Jewish people said "evening and morning" rather than "morning and evening," because their days started with sunset, not sunrise. Thus, sunset on Thursday evening ushered in Friday, and sunset on Friday ushered in the Sabbath day.

9. People who depend on their astrological charts for guidance are following ancient pagan customs that are useless. There's no evidence that the position of the heavenly bodies has any influence on human life on earth. The Bible condemns all human attempts to foresee or control the future (Deut. 18:10–13; Isa. 47:13; Jer. 10:2). The statement that the sun and moon "rule over" the day and night respectively doesn't mean that they exert special influence on the affairs of people but that day and night are their spheres of operation. According to the rotation of the earth, its orbit around the sun, and the moon's orbit around the earth, the sun and moon govern how much light there will be on earth.

10. Ralph Waldo Emerson, *Nature* (Boston: Beacon Press, 1985), 9–10.

11. Even though many animals are stronger than we are and live longer than we do, God has given humans dominion over the animals. However, this doesn't mean we can abuse animal life and do whatever we please with God's creatures (Jer. 27:5). While animals have been given to serve us, we must treat them as creatures made by God. "A

righteous man regards the life of his animal" (Prov. 12:10 NKJV). "Do not muzzle an ox while it is treading out the grain" (Deut. 25:4 NIV). God takes care of the animals (Ps. 36:6; 104:10–18; Matt. 6:26) and knows when they suffer (Joel 1:18–20; 2:22; Jonah 4:11). Even the way we treat helpless birds is a concern to God (Deut. 22:6–7). Those who abuse and exploit God's creation will one day be judged (Rev. 11:18).

12. You have a similar "dialogue" recorded in Genesis 3:22; 11:7, and see Isaiah 6:8.

13. As we have seen, the Hebrew word *ruah* means "breath" and "spirit" (or Spirit). The breath of God brought life to Adam just as the Spirit of God brings eternal life to the sinner who believes on Christ (John 3:7–8; 20:22).

14. Dominion over the earth and its creatures may have been the privilege Lucifer wanted when he rebelled against God and led some of the angels in revolt against the Lord. Isaiah 14:12–17 speaks primarily about the fall of the king of Babylon, but behind this mysterious passage lurks the image of "the son of the morning," the angel who wanted to be as God and promised to make Eve like God (Gen. 3:5).

Chapter Three

1. In Scripture, the number seven often stands for fullness and completion. According to Leviticus 23, the Hebrew calendar was built on a series of sevens. The seventh day of the week was the Sabbath, and Pentecost occurred seven weeks after the Feast of Firstfruits. During the seventh month, the Jews celebrated the Day of Atonement, the Feast of Trumpets, and the Feast of Tabernacles. Each seventh year was a Sabbatical Year and the fiftieth year was the Year of Jubilee.

2. The Hebrew word *qadas* means "to set apart, to make holy" and can be applied to people (Ex. 13:2; 19:14), inanimate objects (29:36–37,

44), events such as fasts (Joel 1:14) and wars (Jer. 6:4 where "prepare" is *qada),* and even the name of God (Ezek. 36:23). That which God sanctifies must never be treated as something common.

3. Our English word "covenant" comes from two Latin words that mean "to come together." A lease on a house enables two parties to come together in a business arrangement. The marriage vows, authorized by a marriage license, enable a man and woman to live together as husband and wife. Without such agreements, society would fall apart.

4. The Tree of Life is a repeated image in Proverbs (3:18; 11:30; 13:12; 15:4) and also in the book of Revelation (2:7; 22:2, 14, 19). The Tree of Life is found in the heavenly "garden city" providing sustenance and healing.

5. In Matthew 19:10–12, Jesus made it clear that not everybody is supposed to be married, although most people expect to be married and probably want to be married. Singleness is not a curse. God gives people different gifts (1 Cor. 7:7) and calls people to tasks commensurate with their gifts. In the church, neither gender nor marital status determine spirituality or fellowship (Gal. 4:26–29).

6. The Song of Songs magnifies the enjoyment of married love and says nothing about conception or children. In ancient Jewish society, it was considered a disgrace not to have children, yet many fine marriages were not blessed with offspring, and such is the case today.

7. The Hebrew says, "She shall be called *ishsha* because she was taken out of *ish.*" Scholars aren't agreed on the significance of *ishsha* as derived from *ish.* Perhaps it's a parallel to the words *adam* (man) and *adama* (ground) in 2:7 and 3:19. Man was made out of the ground; woman was made out of man.

Chapter Four

1. In Psalm 139, after David ponders his being made by God in the womb, he immediately mentions the Word of God (vv. 17–18).

Chapter Five

1. While Satan is certainly at work throughout biblical history, in the Old Testament, he makes four special "personal appearances": to tempt Eve (Gen. 3); to get permission to attack Job (Job 1—2); to tempt David (2 Sam. 24; 1 Chron. 21); and to accuse Joshua the high priest (Zech. 3). For a study of these four passages and what they mean to the church today, see my book *The Strategy of Satan* (Tyndale House). Other books that can help you better understand Satan and his wiles are: *The Voice of the Devil* by G. Campbell Morgan (Baker reprint); *I Believe in Satan's Downfall* by Michael Green (Eerdmans); *Satan: His Motives and Methods* by Lewis Sperry Chafer (Zondervan); *Your Adversary the Devil* by J. Dwight Pentecost (Zondervan); *The Invisible War* by Donald Grey Barnhouse (Zondervan); and *The Adversary* by Mark Bubeck (Moody Press).

2. Samuel Butler, *The Note Books of Samuel Butler,* edited by Henry F. Jones (New York: E. P. Dutton, 1921), 217.

3. Charles Neider, ed., *The Complete Essays of Mark Twain* (Garden City, New York: Doubleday, 1963), 237. Like Butler, Twain says, "We have none but the evidence for the prosecution, and yet we have rendered the verdict."

4. Many students believe that the fall of Satan (Lucifer) lies behind the "taunt song" description of the defeat of the king of Babylon found in Isaiah 14:12–17. John Milton took this view (and embellished it) when he wrote "Paradise Lost."

5. In Genesis 3:1–5, both Satan and Eve use plural pronouns, suggesting that Adam may have been present but said nothing. However, it's

likely that these plural pronouns simply mean that Satan and Eve included Adam because he was the one to whom God originally gave the prohibition about the trees (2:15–17). God used singular pronouns when speaking to Adam, so Eve was told the divine commandment by her husband.

6. Many people who claim to have had "out-of-body" experiences report that they felt no fear because they saw "a bright light at the end of the dark tunnel." Assuming that this light was the presence of God in heaven, they had confidence that they were ready to meet God. But Satan the imitator knows how to produce light and imitate the very angels of God.

7. Eve's innocent response to the words of a talking animal is another argument for the absence of Adam, or else we have to believe that humans and animals were able to communicate in Eden. Since Adam had named all the animals, he would have known the nature of the serpent, that it couldn't speak. Adam has been blamed for not being with his wife, but he had work to do and the garden was probably large. As for Adam's "guarding" the garden, Genesis 2:15 speaks of working and taking care of the garden (NIV). The Hebrew word translated "dress" in the KJV and "take care of" in the NIV can also mean "to watch, to guard" and is translated that way in 3:24 (NIV, NKJV). But since God had pronounced the serpent "good," what reason would Adam have for thinking it was a part of a wicked plan and that his wife was in danger? Without the advantage of hindsight, what would we have done had we been in his place?

8. If Isaiah 14:12–15 is a description of the fall of Satan, then the statement "I will be like the most High" (v. 14) reveals the hidden agenda behind Satan's revolt: He wanted to be like God. He failed in reaching this goal, so now he passes the desire along to Eve in the

form of a promise. Satan desires the worship and service that belong only to the Lord God (Matt. 4:8–10).

9. It's interesting to contrast Genesis 3:8 ("the cool of the day") and 18:1 ("the heat of the day"). God's visit in the garden was to call man to forgiveness, but His visit to Abraham was to announce, among other things, the destruction of the wicked cities of the plain.

10. Note three interesting questions that God asks in Genesis: "Where are you?" (3:9 NIV) "Where is your brother?" (4:9 NIV) and "Where is your wife?" (18:9 NIV)

11. The Greek preface *anti* means both "instead of Christ" (i.e., a false Christ) and "against Christ." There were "antichrists" (false teachers) opposing the church in the first century (1 John 2:18–29), and they are still with us. The test of false teachers is what they teach about the person and work of Jesus Christ.

12. The Hebrew phrase in Genesis 2:17 (NIV) is "dying you will die," which means "you will surely die." But it suggests both a crisis and a process. To die means to be separated from God, which is what happened to our first parents the instant they sinned. But death also means the separation of the spirit from the body (James 2:26), and the process of dying began with their disobedience and ended years later when they expired. Because of the law of sin and death, life has always been a constant battle to conquer death.

13. The first Adam was a thief and was cast out of paradise. The Last Adam, while hanging on the cross, said to a thief, "[T]oday, you will be with Me in Paradise" (Luke 23:43 NKJV).

Chapter Six

1. *As You Like It,* Act 2, scene 7, lines 139–142.

2. It's often been said that if you aren't a child of God, you're automatically a child of the Devil, but I question that evangelical

cliché. Ephesians 2:1–3 teaches that we're born by nature the "children of wrath," and that by choice we become the "children of disobedience." If we reject Christ's righteousness and depend on our own self-righteousness, then we become "children of the devil." See the discussion of Genesis 3:15 in chapter 5, section 5.

3. You find this sequence in 1 John 1:6, 8, and 10.

4. Righteous Abel (Matt. 23:35) speaks to God's people today both by his sacrifices (Heb. 11:4) and by his shed blood (Heb. 12:24). In the latter passage, the writer contrasts the blood of Christ and the blood of Abel. The blood of Abel speaks from the earth, but Christ's blood speaks from heaven. Abel's blood cries out for justice, but Christ's blood speaks of justice satisfied on the cross. Abel's blood declared Cain's guilt and made him a wanderer, but Christ's blood speaks of grace and forgiveness and reconciles believing sinners to God.

5. The plaque outside "The Chamber of Destruction" holocaust museum on Mount Zion in Jerusalem reads, "Listen! Your brother's blood cries out!"

6. We don't know how many people were alive on earth at this time, although we're told that Adam "begat sons and daughters" (Gen. 5:4). Sin had not yet taken its toll in the human body or in the natural world, so people lived longer and probably were more prolific.

7. We must not imagine that Cain's "city" was like our modern cities. It was a settlement of people for mutual help and protection. Some would live in tents and others in more permanent dwellings, and there might be a wall to protect them.

Chapter Seven

1. Some Old Testament scholars warn us against building too strong a case for biblical chronology solely on the basis of the lists found in Genesis 5, 10, and 11. Comparison with other genealogies in

Scripture indicates that these lists may not be complete. The fact
that the genealogies in Genesis 5 and 11 both have ten generations
suggests an artificial pattern. (See also Ruth 4:18–22.) Furthermore,
ancient Semitic peoples used the term "father" to refer to any male
ancestor.

2. The Hebrew word translated "call upon" carries the meaning of
praying in God's name and also proclaiming His name in worship.
The sentence can also be translated "men began to call themselves
by the name of the Lord." All three meanings are probably true: The
believing remnant met to praise God and pray to Him for help, and
in time, they identified themselves as those who bore His name.

3. When you add up the ages of Methuselah, Lamech, and Noah when
their eldest sons were born (187 + 182 + 500), plus the 100 years
between 5:32 and 7:11, you get a total of 969 years.

4. See *Earth's Earliest Ages,* by G. H. Pember (Revell) and the writings
of E. W. Bullinger, especially *The Companion Bible* (The Lamp Press)
and *How to Enjoy the Bible* (London: Eyre and Spottiswoode, 1928).
James M. Gray also espouses the "angel" theory in his *Christian
Workers' Commentary* (Kregel reprint). For *an able refutation* of
the "angel theory," see *Studies in Problem Texts* by J. Sidlow Baxter
(Zondervan). The theory is the result of juggling some puzzling
passages (Jude 6–7; 1 Peter 3:19–20; 2 Peter 2:4–9) and overlooking
some basic principles of hermeneutics.

5. "Sons [children] of God" can also refer to humans. See Deuteronomy
14:1; Psalm 82:6; Isaiah 43:6; Hosea 11:1.

6. God the Father was grieved at man's sin on the earth (Gen. 6:6);
God the Son was grieved by the hardness of heart of religious people
(Mark 3:5); and God the Spirit can be grieved by the sins of the saints
(Eph. 4:30).

Chapter Eight

1. Henry M. Morris, *The Genesis Record* (Baker, 1976), 180ff. See also *The Genesis Flood,* by Henry M. Morris and John C. Whitcomb, Jr. (Baker, 1967), and *Studies in the Bible and Science* by Henry M. Morris (Baker, 1966).

2. The three boys are usually identified as Noah's sons and not by their given names (6:18; 7:7; 8:16, 18; 9:1, 8). We are never told Noah's wife's name or the names of his three daughters-in-law. God's covenant with Noah included all the members of the household.

3. For a fair discussion of both views that leans toward the limited flood interpretation, see *The Book of Genesis: An Introductory Commentary,* by Ronald F. Youngblood (Baker, 1991; second edition), chapter 10.

4. While it's true that the Hebrew word for "earth" can also mean "land," "land" doesn't fit with the universal statements in the text, such as 6:12–13 where God promises to wipe out "all flesh," and 7:4, "every living substance."

5. To argue that the building of the ark was a "witness to the people" is to ignore what God had to say about the ark, that its purpose was to keep humans and animals alive during the flood (6:19–20; 7:23). Although the building of the ark surely attracted attention, there's no mention in the text of the ark serving as a witness to the lost.

6. New Testament baptism was by immersion, picturing the believer's identification with Christ in death, burial, and resurrection (Rom. 6).

7. Alexander Maclaren, *Expositions of Holy Scripture* (Baker, 1974), vol. 1, 84.

Chapter Nine

1. Moses took this approach when he interceded with God for sinful Israel: "Remember Abraham, Isaac, and Israel" (Ex. 32:13), and it was Nehemiah's repeated prayer (Neh. 13:14, 22, 29, 31). To ask

God to remember is to remind Him of His promises and claim those promises for yourself (Ps. 25:6–7; 105:8, 42; 106:4, 45; 132:1; 136:23). Mary rejoiced in God's remembrance of His mercy (Luke 1:54–55), and Zacharias sang about it at the birth of John the Baptist (Luke 1:72–73). The name Zacharias means "God remembers."

2. To review God's special concern for animals, read note 11 in chapter 2.

3. See Genesis 28:15; Deuteronomy 4:31; 31:6; Joshua 1:5; 1 Kings 8:57; 1 Chronicles 28:9, 20; Isaiah 42:16; Matthew 28:20; Hebrews 13:5.

4. Kay Orr, when Governor of Nebraska, made me an Admiral of the Nebraska Navy. When I asked a long-time resident why Nebraska had a navy, he explained that the state is sitting on "an ocean of water," which explains the extensive farm irrigation system that you see as you drive on I-80. Nebraska also has some of the richest "digs" for finding the remains of prehistoric animals. Is this something we should attribute to the flood? Perhaps.

5. Beginning with the Exodus, the Jews had both civil and religious calendars. The civil year began in the seventh month (Tishri), our mid-September to mid-October; but the religious year started with Passover, the fourteenth day of Nisan (Ex. 12:2), our mid-March to mid-April. However, Nisan would be the seventh month of the *civil* year, and the seventeenth day of the seventh month would be three days after Passover, *the day of our Lord's resurrection.* This explains why Peter associated the ark with the resurrection of Jesus Christ (1 Peter 3:18–22), for the ark rested in Ararat on the date our Lord arose from the dead.

6. Ever since the days of the church fathers, preachers have seen the two birds as illustrations of the two natures (and two appetites) in the child of God, the flesh and the spirit (Gal. 5:16–26). The dove certainly typifies the Spirit of God (Matt. 3:16).

7. God's concern is for the salvation and devotion of the entire family, and that's why He instructed the Jewish fathers and mothers to teach the Word to their children. See Deuteronomy 6:4–9 and Psalms 78:1–8; 102:28; 103:17–18; 112:1–2. At Pentecost, Peter declared that God's promise included the children so that they too could believe and be saved (Acts 2:38–39), and Paul gave the same assurance to the Philippian jailer (16:31). We can't believe for our children, but we can prepare the way for our children to believe.

8. The burnt offering also involved atonement for sin (Lev. 1:4; Job 1:5) and thanksgiving to God.

9. It was God who provided the sacrifices because He commanded Noah to take the clean animals with him on the ark (Gen. 7:2–3). What we give to God, He has first given to us (1 Chron. 29:14), and we don't give to God because He lacks anything (Ps. 50:7–15) or needs anything (Acts 17:24–25). Our giving brings delight to God, but it doesn't enrich God personally. Rather, giving enriches the worshipper (Phil. 4:18).

Chapter Ten

1. Roy B. Zuck, *Precious in His Sight: Childhood and Children in the Bible* (Baker, 1996), 71. This book ought to be read by every parent, pastor, children's worker, and teacher of children.

2. "But you must not eat flesh from a still-living animal" is the way Stephen Mitchell translates Genesis 9:4 in *Genesis: A New Translation of the Classic Biblical Stories* (New York: HarperCollins, 1996), 17. Since the blood is the life, then flesh with blood still in it is considered living flesh.

3. The issue at the Acts 15 Jerusalem consultation was not health but theology: Must a Gentile become a Jew in order to become a Christian? The answer, of course, was a resounding no. The related

question Paul dealt with in Romans 14—15 was, "Must a Christian live like a Jew in order to be a good Christian?" This was a matter of personal love: Do nothing that would cause weaker Christians to stumble, but don't let them stay weak. Help them to see the truth and have the faith to obey it.

4. According to the law of Moses, if an animal killed a human, the animal was to be killed. If the animal was known to be dangerous but wasn't penned up, then the owner of the animal was in danger of losing his life. See Exodus 21:28–32.

5. For a biblical study of capital punishment, see *On Capital Punishment,* by William H. Baker (Chicago: Moody Press, 1985). See also C. S. Lewis' masterful essay "The Humanitarian Theory of Punishment" in *God in the Dock: Essays on Theology and Ethics,* edited by Walter Hooper (Grand Rapids: Eerdmans, 1970), 287–94.

6. Psalm 104 emphasizes that all creation depends on God and worships God, including the beasts of the field (vv. 11, 21), the fowl (vv. 12, 17), the cattle (v. 14), and mankind (vv. 14, 23).

7. Richard K. Curtis, *They Called Him Mister Moody* (Grand Rapids: Eerdmans, 1967), 53.

Chapter Eleven

1. Russell Baker, "Life With Mother" in *Inventing the Truth,* edited by William Zinsser (New York: Book-of-the-Month Club, 1987), 49.

2. Exodus 20:5–6 and 34:7 balance this principle: God does punish the children for their father's sins *if the sins of the fathers are repeated by the children,* and this frequently happens. Whether it's because of inherited genetic weakness or the influence of bad examples, children sometimes follow in their parents' footsteps.

3. Some students see this "service" not as slavery but as rendering service to others, and perhaps this idea is included in Noah's statement. Some

of the Hamitic civilizations contributed much to the material and intellectual progress of the world.

4. In view of what happened to Noah, it's significant that the word "nakedness" is found twenty-four times in this chapter. To "uncover nakedness" means, of course, to have sexual relations with a person, which is the way the NIV translates it.

5. This is not the modern Ethiopia but an African nation usually identified as "Cush" in modern translations. Cush was a son of Ham.

6. We've already noticed lists of ten generations from Adam to Noah (Gen. 5), from Shem to Abraham (11:10–26), and from Perez to David (Ruth 4:18–22). Matthew's genealogy of our Lord follows a pattern of three sets of fourteen generations each, from Abraham to Christ (Matt. 1:1–17). Deuteronomy 32:8 states that the division of the nations was "according to the number of the children of Israel." Does this refer to the seventy people in Jacob's (Israel's) family? Some texts read "the number of the sons of God," which may refer to the angels, since Jewish tradition said there were seventy "territorial angels" and each was assigned to a nation (Dan. 10:12–21).

7. I once saw a sporting goods store that was named "Rod and Nimrod," suggesting that they sold equipment for both fishermen and hunters.

8. It's possible that the name "Hebrew" comes from "Eber," but not all Hebraists agree. Some connect "Hebrew" with a word meaning "to pass through or over," that is, "from beyond the other side," meaning "a wanderer, a stranger." Abraham the alien was called "the Hebrew" (Gen. 14:13), as was Joseph in Egypt (39:14; 41:12; 43:32).

9. In 1868, Robert S. Candlish proposed an interesting interpretation of this puzzling verse. He suggested that God told Eber how to divide the various nations and where to send them. Nimrod was attempting to consolidate the peoples under his rule, but God

thwarted his efforts by dispersing the various clans. See *Studies in Genesis* by Robert S. Candlish (Grand Rapids: Kregel Publications, 1979), 172–73.

10. Dr. A. T. Pierson often said "History is His story."

Chapter Twelve

1. Even where people speak the same language, they may also use different local dialects, and the same words can have different meanings in different places. George Bernard Shaw is supposed to have said that England and America are two countries divided by a common language.

2. Beard was paraphrasing a statement from the Greek dramatist Sophocles: "Whom Zeus would destroy, he first makes mad." This statement became a proverb and versions of it have appeared in many languages.

3. Naomi H. Rosenblatt and Joshua Horowitz, *Wrestling with Angels* (New York: Dell Publishing, 1995), 82.

4. This isn't to suggest that all global technology and worldwide megacorporations are necessarily evil in themselves. It's the spirit and purpose of these "towers" that the Christian must avoid. "Be not conformed to this world" (Rom. 12:2). "And the world is passing away, and the lust of it; but he who does the will of God abides forever" (1 John 2:17 NKJV). God's people can make good use of global technology to spread the gospel and build the church, but our faith must be in God and our purpose must be to glorify God. The Bible repeatedly warns believers not to be so identified with the world system that they share in its ultimate judgment (Isa. 48:20; Jer. 50:8; 51:6, 45; 1 Cor. 11:32; Rev. 18:4).

5. See *Technopoly: The Surrender of Culture to Technology* by Neil Postman (New York: Knopf, 1992; reprint, Vintage Books, 1993);

and *The Technological Bluff* by Jacques Ellul (Grand Rapids: Eerdmans, 1990).

6. God changed Abram's and Sarah's names to Abraham and Sarah, respectively, in Genesis 17:1–17.

Chapter Thirteen

1. It's unfortunate that some people have made an issue over what pronouns we should use when referring to God. The Bible consistently uses "he," but not because the male gender is more godlike. God is spirit, and spirit beings (including angels) have no gender. For some reason, people who object to God being called "he" don't object when Satan is called "he"; yet Satan is also a spirit creature who is sexless.